Nathaniel Dimock

Dangerous deceits

An examination of the teaching of our Article Thirty-one

Nathaniel Dimock

Dangerous deceits
An examination of the teaching of our Article Thirty-one

ISBN/EAN: 9783337163839

Printed in Europe, USA, Canada, Australia, Japan

Cover: Foto ©Paul-Georg Meister /pixelio.de

More available books at **www.hansebooks.com**

'DANGEROUS DECEITS

AN EXAMINATION

OF

The Teaching of our Article Thirty-one.

BY

REV. N. DIMOCK, A.M.

LONDON:
ELLIOT STOCK, 62, PATERNOSTER ROW, E.C
1895.

INTRODUCTION.

THE aim of the following paper is a very simple one.

It has not been written with any desire to forge, or to fasten, or to tighten, fetters for the clergy of the Church of England.

The writer, indeed, may think that some of his friends, who (with himself) are grieved for the divisions of Christendom, may need a word of warning against imagining that there can ever be reunion with the Roman obedience, until either Rome shall be 'other than she is'—which the kindly letter of the Pope gives small ground for expecting—or the Church of England shall be faithless to the principles of her Reformation—which may God, in His mercy, forbid!

He may be deeply convinced himself, and earnestly desirous that others should be convinced, that true healthful comprehensiveness can never desire anything so destructive of all comprehension as the removing of landmarks and the breaking down of fences for the very purpose of including the comprehension of essential and vital antagonisms.

But the purpose of this pamphlet is limited to the work of clearing the true sense of one of our Articles, the

Article which was formerly understood as saying its emphatic 'Nay' to the doctrine of the Mass.

The writer's desire has been to show that those among us who are persuaded that the 'Nay' of our Reformers has been learnt from the teaching of God's Word and the truth of Christ's Gospel, while the 'Yea' of the Mass-sacrifice has come of the teaching for doctrines the commandments of men, have the plain words of the Article on their side, and that, in their appeal to the teaching of the Article, they have no need to tremble for the truth of their convictions by reason of certain recent attempts to mine their position.

The writer desires to add that he is far from desiring to imply that those whose views in this matter he is constrained to oppose are all of them upholders of the Roman doctrine. Of some he believes, of others he hopes, that in view of the doctrine of the Mass *as he understands it*, they would be as ready as himself to oppose its dangerous deceits.

May the God of Love, the God of Truth, the God of Peace, bring loving hearts together in the bond of Peace, through the knowledge of THE TRUTH taught by the Mighty Power of the Spirit of Truth!

'DANGEROUS DECEITS.'

WEIGHTY considerations have been urgently calling for something like a re-examination of the doctrine contained in our 31st Article. It is being widely taught, and by some whose names carry weight, and by some who are far from being upholders of Tridentine doctrine, that it was and is intended to condemn no Romish doctrine whatever, but only certain grievous abuses of the Mass which were more or less prevalent before the Reformation. It seems to be believed by not a few that some new light has recently been thrown upon the subject tending to give material support to this contention. And there are probably many, quite free from any Romeward tendencies, who are not indisposed to accept and welcome this teaching, as seeming to relieve them from the necessity of upholding language which, as applied to the common belief of so large and influential a portion of Christendom, might seem to be needlessly offensive, if not lacking in charity. They would gladly believe that such terms as 'blasphemous fables and dangerous deceits' were fitly applied only to an obscure and now obsolete form of the grossest superstition, and that there is nothing in the true doctrinal system of Rome to which they can justly be applicable.

The aim of the present paper is briefly but fairly to discuss this subject, and to weigh the arguments adduced in the balances of truth.

1. We must begin with the very words of the Article. For all historical arguments are secondary and subservient to those which pertain to the fair interpretation of the language of a document. This statement rests on an axiom which has its roots not more in legal principles than in dictates of common sense. A written document aims, or should aim, at making its meaning sufficiently intelligible in itself. What it does say should be so said that its true sense may be naturally read out of it. And what it does not say should not, by force of external reasoning, be read into it. This does not indeed require us to order all historical evidence out of court. Such evidence may at times be important and valuable. But its highest value will commonly consist in throwing light on expressions

which may have been sufficiently clear at the date of the document's composition, but which changes in language, or customs, or circumstances may have made less easy of interpretation in our own day.

(*a*) We begin, then, with a very obvious observation. When the Article speaks of the teaching which it has in view as that which 'was commonly said,' it can hardly be supposed to be aiming at anything which had attained to the position of an authoritative doctrine in the Romish Church. Why use such an expression 'quibus vulgo dicebatur' of any teaching which was recognised as the true teaching of Romanists? It may certainly be fairly argued that the language of the Article implies that what is under its condemnation is nothing more than a prevalent floating notion concerning the efficacy of the Mass, by which popular opinion had been in danger of being grievously deceived.

But, then, it is to be remembered that at the date of the putting forth of this Article in 1553, there was absolutely no authoritative statement of the doctrine of the Mass.[1] The growth of

[1] It could not be fastened on the Mass-Book, which contains no verbal oblation of Christ. Indeed, the Reformers (though sometimes dealing unsparingly with Roman Canon as interpreted in the Roman sense) were accustomed to appeal to the Missal against the Mass.

doctrine in the Romish communion seems ever to have been somewhat after this manner. A new notion, resting perhaps on some 'pious excess of language' in earlier days, takes hold on men's minds; it spreads, it establishes itself as a common opinion, it works itself into Rome's popular system, it becomes 'commonly said,' and then, finally, it receives authoritative confirmation in some form or other. It was therefore impossible for our Article to designate the doctrine it opposed in any other way than it did. It had come now to be the commonly received opinion. It had not yet been stamped with any ecclesiastical authority.

The question before Europe at that date was—Would the Council of Trent also condemn what our Article condemns, or would it uphold and maintain what had been so 'commonly said'?

And the question before us now is—Has the Council, or has it not, set its seal to that doctrine which the Article has marked as a popular error?

(b) But before we proceed to compare the language of the Article with that of the Tridentine Canon, it will be well to notice another verbal argument which has been urged to shield the doctrine of Rome from the intention of the

Article. It rests on[1] the use of the plural number 'Sacrifices of Masses.' It is urged that the doctrine which Rome teaches could only be rightly described as the 'Sacrifice of the Mass' in the singular.

We can hardly believe that much weight is attached to this argument by its advocates. It is true, indeed, that, from a certain point of view, or in a certain limited sense, Romish Divines are found maintaining that the Sacrifice of the Mass is one and the same with the Sacrifice of the Cross—that there are not many sacrifices, but one only sacrifice. But from another point of view, or in another sense,[2] it is usual with them

[1] See Dr. Pusey's 'Eirenicon,' p. 25. Possibly the argument (though made something of in Bishop Wordsworth's 'Responsio ad Batavos,' p. 6) is now generally abandoned. Canon Gore says: 'The Church offers many sacrifices, many as are her altars, her churches, her priests and people, many as are the days of the year; but all these many sacrifices gain their power and their acceptance when, through mystical consecration of the Spirit, they are taken up into union with Christ's Eternal Sacrifice' ('The Euch. Sacr.,' pp. 11, 12).

[2] The hostia offered is the same, and the High Priest who offers is the same, the difference being only in the mode of offering. But the Act of Oblation is in each Mass distinct, and this act is of the essence of the sacrifice, according to Bellarmine, 'Nam non res illa, sed illius oblatio proprie sacrificium est; sacrificium enim est actio, non res permanens' ('De Missa,' Lib. II., cap. iv.; 'De Contro,' tom. iii., c. 1,054; Ingols. 1601), though else-

to speak of Masses in the plural, and of the Church's sacrifices as many. And this language, which prevailed before the Council of Trent, has been not less common since. Indeed, the Council itself uses the plural number. Witness the following : ' Nec tamen . . . missas illas in quibus solus sacerdos sacramentaliter communicat, ut privatas et illicitas damnat [synodus], sed probat, atque adeo commendat' (Sess. XXII., cap. vi.). ' Si quis dixerit, imposturam esse, missas celebrare in honorem sanctorum, et pro illorum intercessione apud Deum obtinenda, sicut Ecclesia intendit : anathema sit' (Sess. XXII., Canon V.). ' Si quis dixerit, missas in quibus solus sacerdos sacramentaliter communicat, illicitas esse, ideoque abrogandas : anathema sit' (Sess. XXII., Canon VIII.). So also the Catechism of the Council of Trent, ' Ex quo facile perspicitur omnes missas communes esse ; ut quæ ad communem omnium fidelium utilitatem et salutem

---

where (c. 1006) he acknowledges the ambiguity of the term. Compare the following : ' Oblatio sine quâ non potest fieri Sacrificium, cum omne Sacrificium sit oblatio ' (Judicium D. R. Tapperi, Decani Lovaniensis, De Sacr. Miss. In Le Plat, Mon. ad h. Conc. Trid., tom. iv., p. 340).

Other authorities differ. Pighius, *e.g.*, declares : ' Nec ipse offerendi actus, sed id quod Deo offertur, est sacrificium.' (In ' Contro. Ratisb.,' f. 119, *a.*)

The Tridentine Catechism teaches ' Sacrificii vis in eo est, ut offeratur.' (Cf. Dens, 'Tract. Theol.,' p. 366. Dublin, 1812.)

pertineant' (Pars II., cap. iv., § lxxxvii.). The plural is used also in cap. iii.

Indeed, it needs but a moderate acquaintance with the writings of approved Divines in the Romish Church to notice how, not only are 'Masses' habitually spoken of in the plural, but *repetition* and *iteration* are frequently attributed to the sacrifice of the altar.[1]

(c) But a further argument is urged from the teaching of the Article itself, which ought to receive careful consideration.

The first division of the Article is a declaration of the sufficiency of the 'oblatio Christi semel facta' ('the offering of Christ made once for ever,' 1553), and what in the second division is stated concerning the Sacrifices of Masses is connected with this declaration as its necessary consequent. '*Unde* (wherefore) Missarum sacrificia . . . figmenta sunt.' It follows that the teaching condemned must be a teaching which is inconsistent with the previous declaration, or, in other words, a doctrine which derogates from the perfection and sufficiency of Christ's sacrifice on the Cross. But, it is urged, the Romish doctrine of the Mass, as rightly understood, does in no wise derogate from the perfect redemption, propitiation, and satisfaction of Christ's offering

[1] See Appendix, Note A.

once made. Therefore the teaching meant to be under the Article's condemnation cannot be the doctrine of the Mass, but must be some popular abuse or vulgar misrepresentation of that doctrine.

Against this it must be said that the argument begs a most important question. Does the doctrine of Mass, as taught by the Church of Rome, or does it not, derogate from the all-sufficiency of the sacrifice of the Death of Christ? Of course, Romish Divines maintain that it does not. But the argument we are dealing with has no force at all unless it can be shown that it is impossible for the Church of England to have differed herein from the Church of Rome; whereas it is notorious that the Reformers, English as well as continental, after the determination of the Council of Trent on the subject as well as before, were of one mind in regarding the Romish doctrine of the Mass as irreconcileable with the Scriptural view of the Atonement of the Sacrifice of Christ. Herein they were followed by the great Divines of the Church of England in after generations.

These Divines were not ignorant of the Romish methods of reconciling the doctrine of the Mass with the Sacrifice of the Cross. Is it quite impossible to believe that they were right in regarding them as shifts and evasions? In view of the inspired authority for the deduction from the truth of the perfection of Christ's sacrifice—'there is no more offering for sin' (Heb. x. 18, 26)—is it quite certain they were wrong in deducing from the same truth the assurance that there can be *therefore* (*unde*) no room for the sacrifices of masses?

If further rebutting evidence were needed, it might be found in the teaching of the larger Catechism of Nowel, who acted as Prolocutor in the Convocation which revised and authorized the 'Articles of Religion' after the Council of Trent had defined the doctrine of the Mass. It is the Catechism referred to in our 79th Canon of 1603, which says : 'All schoolmasters shall teach in English or Latin, as the children are able to bear, the larger or shorter Catechism heretofore by public authority set forth.'

The following extract speaks to the point :
'M. Ex iis quæ jam de Cœna Dominica commemorasti, videor mihi . colligere, eam non in hunc finem institutam esse, ut Christi Corpus Deo Patri pro peccatis in sacrificium offeratur.

'A. Minime vero ita offertur. Nam ipse ut Corpore suo vescamur, non ut illud offeramus, cum Cœnam suam institueret, præcepit. Offerendi vero pro peccatis prærogativa ad solum

Christum, ut qui æternus ille sit sacerdos, pertinet, qui et unicum illud perpetuumque sacrificium moriens in Cruce pro salute nostra semel fecit, illique abunde in omne tempus satisfecit. Nobis vero nihil restat, nisi ut æterni illius sacrificii usum fructum nobis ab ipso Domino legatum gratis animis capiamus : quod quidem in Cœna Dominica maxime facimus.

'M. Sacra igitur Cœna, ut video, ad mortem Christi, ejusque in Cruce perpetratum semel sacrificium, quo solo placatus nobis Deus efficitur, nos remittit.' (p. 174 ; Edit. Jacobson).

If there were no other evidence to the point, surely this would suffice to show that, so far as the Church of England has approved the teaching of Nowel's Catechism,[1] so far also she approves of the teaching that the sacrifice of the Mass is a derogation from the doctrine of the full and perfect sacrifice of Christ. But that it is impossible that she can mean to approve of such teaching is the very foundation of the argument that the 31st Article (by reason of its connecting *unde*) must point to some other doctrine than the Romish doctrine of the Mass.[2]

[1] On the sanction given to Nowel's Catechism, see papers on the 'Eucharistic Presence,' pp. 187-191.

[2] The same conclusion might, with much probability at least, have been inferred from the introduction (in the prayer of consecration) of the words ' Who made there (by His one

(*d*) Before we go further there remains yet another argument resting on the language of the Articles.

It is pressed upon us that the very strength of the language used ('blasphemous fables and dangerous deceits') must surely lead to the conclusion that some gross corruption of doctrine, not the very doctrine of the Mass itself, is here in view.

But the answer to this is simple and obvious. If it was possible that the Church of England regarded (as the Reformers regarded) the very doctrine of the Mass itself as a derogation from the perfection of the Sacrifice of the Cross, then it is surely quite credible that she may have thought (as our Reformers certainly thought) that the doctrine warranted, and even called for, such strong language of condemnation. Will anyone maintain that, on the hypothesis of this charge against the Mass being true, such language would not be justifiable? Certainly the like

---

oblation once offered) a full, perfect, and sufficient sacrifice,' etc., in the place of the Sarum oblation. Canon Estcourt says of this that 'having been substituted in place of the "Hanc oblationem servitutis nostræ placatus accipias," it can only mean that the sacrifice of the Mass is derogatory to Christ's sacrifice on the Cross, and that the Eucharistic sacrifice is a bare commemoration of His death, but not a propitiatory sacrifice' ('Dogmatic Teaching,' p. 54).

expressions will be found, as applied to the doctrine of the Romish Mass, and even stronger language sometimes, not only in the teachings of our English Reformers, nor only in the works of Puritan Divines, but in the writings of esteemed men of the Anglo-Catholic School of a more advanced theology.[1]

(*e*) It only now remains for us, under this head, to compare the language used by the Article to describe the doctrine it condemns with the language used by the Council of Trent to describe the doctrine it upholds, and to judge whether or not there is substantial agreement between them.

We may observe three particulars concerning the doctrine at which the Article is aimed.

(1.) It is a doctrine which teaches an offering of Christ.

(2.) And this offering is an offering for the quick and the dead (*pro vivis et defunctis*).

(3.) And that for the purpose of their having remission of pain or guilt (*in remissionem pœnæ aut culpæ*).

(1.) We ask, then, concerning the *first* particular—Does the doctrine upheld by the Council of Trent agree with this description? On this point, indeed, the answer is too clear to admit of a

[1] See Appendix, Note B.

doubt. In Sess. XXII., cap. ii., we read :
'Quoniam in divino hoc sacrificio, quod in missa
peragitur ; idem ille Christus continetur, et in-
cruente immolatur, qui in ara Crucis semel
seipsum cruente obtulit, docet sancta synodus,'
etc.

(2.) Then as to the second particular. Does
the Council of Trent recognise in the Mass an
offering for the quick and the dead ? The answer
to this also is equally unequivocal. Under the
same chapter we read : ' Non solum pro fidelium
vivorum peccatis, pœnis, satisfactionibus,[1] et aliis

[1] 'Satisfaction is a work which justice requireth to be
done for contentment of persons injured; neither is it in
the eye of justice a sufficient satisfaction, unless it fully
equal the injury for which we satisfy. Seeing, then, that
sin against God eternal and infinite must needs be an
infinite wrong, justice in regard thereof doth necessarily
exact an infinite recompense, or else inflicts on the offender
an infinite punishment. Now, because God was thus to be
satisfied, and man not able to make satisfaction in such
sort, his unspeakable love and inclination to save mankind
from eternal death ordained in our behalf a Mediator to do
that which had been for any other impossible. Wherefore
all sin is remitted in the only faith of Christ's passion,
and no man without belief thereof justified. Faith alone
maketh Christ's satisfaction ours, howbeit that faith alone,
which, after sin, maketh us, by conversion, His.' (Hooker,
' Ecc. Pol.,' Book VI., § 5 ; Works, vol. iii., pp. 56, 57.
Edit. Keble.)

It should, however, be noted that there is a lower sense
in which the word ' satisfaction ' is often used in the
Theology of Rome. See, *e.g.*, Hooker's Works, vol. iii.,

necessitatibus, sed et pro defunctis in Christo nondum ad plenum purgatis, rite, juxta apostolorum traditionem, offertur.'

(3.) The agreement of the Romish doctrine under the third particular is perhaps somewhat less obvious. Yet a little examination can hardly fail to reveal a substantial identity of that which is taught.

The Article says, 'in remissionem pœnæ aut culpæ.'[1] The Council says, 'pro . . . peccatis, pœnis, satisfactionibus.' That which is lacking in verbal agreement ('in remissionem') is made up by the earlier language of the same chapter, which declares : 'Hujus oblatione placatus Dominus, et gratiam et donum pœnitentiæ concedens, crimina et peccata, etiam ingentia, *dimittit*.'[2]

---

p. 489. And in this lower sense it is commonly applied to the Mass Sacrifice.

There is also another sense in which the word is often used by the Fathers. (*Ibid.*, p. 55, *sqq*.)

For a clear exposition of the scholastic idea of satisfaction see Bishop Creighton's 'History of Papacy,' vol. v., p. 59, *sqq*. See also Elliott's 'Delineation of Roman Catholicism,' Book II., ch. xi. The word was doubtless used in the scholastic sense in the canons of the Council of Trent. But in our Article it obviously bears its fullest meaning. And it must be clearly understood with the same fulness of meaning in the Tridentine Catechism, Part.II., cap. iv., § lxxviii.

[1] See Appendix, Note C.

[2] If it should be objected that 'dimittit' may convey a

But it should be further noted that the *unde* of the Article requires us to understand the words 'in remissionem' as having an explanatory correspondence with the '*propitiatio* et satisfactio' of the preceding division, while the Council in its Canon III. distinctly claims for the Sacrifice of the Mass a propitiatory character, condemning those who may regard it as only a sacrifice of praise, or commemoration 'non autem propitiatorium.'[1]

meaning not equivalent to that conveyed by 'to have remission,' it may be answered that in the scholastic distinction between 'dimittere' and 'remittere,' it is 'dimittere' which has the fullest signification. Richardus de Sancto Vict. says: 'Peccata dimittere, hoc est ex toto indulgere. Peccata vero remittere, hoc est debitam eis pœnam temperare, et ex majori parte relaxare ... Vides certe quod multum sit inter remittere atque dimittere ... Remittendi potius quam dimittendi potestas confertur in eo quod dicitur, *Quorum remiseritis peccata remittuntur eis.*' ('De potestate ligandi et solvendi,' cap. xxiv., Op., Part I., p. 522. Colon., 1621.)

[1] It should be observed that here was a clear condemnation in terms of those who had previously defended the Church of Rome by rejecting what was indefensible and maintaining (as Gropper in the *Antididagma*): 'Missam forte appellari posse propitiatorium sacrificium, non quod *vere sit tale*, sed quod sit imago unici propitiatorii sacrificii semel in cruce oblati,' and who had regarded it as a great injustice that they had been accused of teaching 'Missam esse propitiatorium sacrificium pro peccatis.' (See Chemnitz, Exam. Conc. Trid., 'De Mis. Pont.,' Art. IV., pp. 385, 386. Berlin, 1861. See also 'Romish Mass and English Church,' p. 29.)

And, still further, it should be well observed that the Article as issued in 1553, instead of the word 'propitiation' in the English version, had the expression 'the pacifying of God's displeasure,' which was to be attributed to the one Sacrifice of Christ once offered ; and that the Council of Trent attributes just this 'pacifying of God's displeasure' to the Sacrifice of the Mass, in the words 'Hujus quippe oblatione placatus Dominus'—words which again are taken up by the Catechism of Nowel, when it is said of the Sacrifice of the Cross, 'Quo *solo* placatus nobis Deus efficitur.'

What must we say, then, of the relation one to another of the doctrine rejected by our Article, and the doctrine upheld by the Council ? We are constrained to say they are in complete harmony. The verbal agreement might be more exact. The substantial identity is clearly established.[1]

2. We turn now to the consideration of some historical arguments. We need, indeed, to be on our guard against attaching to these an exag-

---

[1] The language of Lingard clearly shows how the Article was naturally regarded from a Roman Catholic point of view (vol. vi., pp. 333, 334). The language of Davenport and Du Pin gives evidence of the difficulties which Roman Catholics found in attempts to read into it the unnatural sense, which alone could bring it into anything like harmony with Roman doctrine.

gerated importance. There is perhaps a tendency in our day to give them a weight beyond what is their due. If our position as fortified by the very language of the Article is really unassailable on that side, it must not be supposed that it can ever be taken by assault from the side of history.

Nevertheless, we desire that a fair and full investigation should be afforded to certain statements which have recently had much prominence given them, and which seem to have made a considerable impression on the public mind.

It is alleged, if we understand the argument aright, that, at the date of the Reformation, a very gross misconception of the doctrine of the Mass had assumed a very definite shape, which may be seen even in the writings of some eminent teachers; that this, having taken a strong hold on popular superstitious tendencies, was the dangerous doctrine which roused the righteous indignation of the Reformers, and that this stands altogether apart, and is clearly to be distinguished from, the doctrine of the Eucharistic Sacrifice which, under the name of the Mass, was maintained by the true theology of the Romish Church. It is urged, further, that this view of the case receives substantial support from the language of the Confession of Augsburg, which is acknowledged to have made its influence felt on our English Reformation.[1]

There is undeniably a foundation of truth underlying all these statements concerning this mediæval teaching of a very gross form of error connected with the doctrine of the Mass. It is true there was abroad a very gross misconception leading to a very grievous superstition which is distinct from, and really irreconcilable with, Rome's recognised teaching concerning the sacrifice.

According to this misconception, it was dreamt that the offering of Christ on the cross availed indeed to take away original sin; but that the sacrifice of Christ in the Mass was that which ought to be looked to as availing to take away the actual sins of baptized Christians.

A doctrine nearly resembling this had received support from somewhat in the writings attributed to Albertus Magnus.[2] But it was more commonly connected with the name of his greater disciple, Thomas Aquinas,[3] who, however, must

---

[1] In the Thirteen Articles of 1538 (through which the Lutheran influence is supposed to have been mainly derived to our Articles of 1553) there is nothing which bears directly on the Mass sacrifice.

[2] See Appendix, Note D.

[3] The same 'Sermones' ('De S. Euch. Sacr.') are found in the printed works of both these doctors.

not for a moment be supposed to have consistently maintained any such doctrine in its grosser form, unclothed with limiting explanations.[1] At the time of the Reformation it found (in some sense) an advocate in Ambrogio Catharino, a Divine, who died in 1553, but who had a place in earlier sessions of the Council of Trent.[2] It was commented upon in the Augsburg Confession. It was certainly not unknown in England, though there seems to be something like a conspicuous lack of evidence to show that it had ever strongly rooted itself in English soil.[3]

---

[1] See Appendix, Note E.

[2] In the session held February 4, 1546, the sermon was preached by Catharinus. See Waterworth's 'Council of Trent,' p. lxxxi.

His sayings and writings are not unfrequently referred to by our Reformers.

He was a Benedictine, Bishop of Minori, afterwards Archbishop of Conza.

[3] The nearest approach to such evidence is probably to be found in the words of Becon: 'The Mass-monger is so impudent and mad that he shameth nothing at all openly to teach, and to blow into all men's ears, that . . . it is no less healthful, profitable, and necessary for the salvation of mankind, than the very passion and death of Christ (" The second cause," saith Thomas of Aquine, " of the institution of the Sacrament of the Altar is the self-sacrifice of the altar against a certain daily robbery of our sins, that, as the body of the Lord was once offered on the cross for original sin, so likewise it should be offered continually for our daily sins upon the altar, and that the Church should have in this behalf a gift to pacify God, precious and acceptable above

It is made mention of by Bishop Jewel, in his controversy with Harding, as an opinion which had been upheld by foreign Divines. But it is seldom alluded to in the writings of our English Reformers. Still, there seems no reason to doubt that it is pointed at in our own Thirty-nine Articles.[1]

But, as in answer to the force of the argument which is built up on all this, it must be observed that—

---

all the sacrifices of the law "), which doctrine, how horrible it is, how uncomely it is, and too much contrary to the doctrine of Christ, yea, what a most pernicious pestilence it is to the salvation of mankind, who is so blind that seeth not?' (Works, 'Prayers,' etc., p. 377. P.S. Edit.) Similar language will be found also in p. 368.

It will be observed that Becon relies on the language of Aquinas. It need not, however, be questioned that the poison of this teaching, and of superstitious doctrines more or less nearly resembling this, had made its influence felt in England. It would have been strange if it had been otherwise.

Bishop J. Wordsworth ('Responsio ad Batavos,' p. 8) refers to Cranmer (on 'Lord's Supper,' pp. 361, 362) and Jewel ('Answer to Harding,' Arts. xix. and xx.), where, however, the language used does not seem to point very definitely to 'the error of Thomas.'

[1] See Articles II. and XXXI. It is scarcely possible to suppose that the treatise of Catharinus 'De veritate incruenti sacrificii' was known in England when our Articles were put forth. It appears to have been published in the latter half of the year 1552. See Bishop J. Wordsworth, 'Responsio ad Batavos,' p. 23.

(*a*) The very distinctness of form which this superstition had assumed makes it all the more difficult—not to say impossible—to believe that this is the teaching which is aimed at in our Article. If the Article had meant this, how are we to account for the fact that it does not describe this, when it could so easily have been described, and in description so easily separated from the true Mass doctrine?

There is in the doctrine which is described in the Article not one of the distinguishing features of this gross superstition. The doctrine described in the Article has a strict correspondence with the doctrine afterwards defined as Rome's doctrine in the Council of Trent. And Rome's doctrine is rightly declared to be clearly separated and distinguished from this corruption. Indeed, it does not appear, so far as we know, that this grievous abuse—notwithstanding the presence of Catharinus—ever even ventured to make its voice heard in the Romish Council.

English Divines were well aware of the abuses which had clung to the Mass doctrine. They may have urged the liability to abuse (which their opponents sometimes denied), even to such a gross abuse as that fathered on Aquinas, as an argument against the Mass itself. But they knew well enough to distinguish between the doctrine and its abuses. And the English Article is levelled, not against an abuse, but against the very doctrine which was so liable to abuse. The Confession, indeed, which was presented at the Diet of Augsburg did clearly aim a blow at this abuse, which it also distinctly described. But it has been long ago pointed out that a comparison of English formularies with Lutheran confessions is instructive not more in respect of points of agreement then in respect of points of divergence. If our English Article had been aimed at the abuse, that abuse would have been unmistakably described, as it had been described in the 'Confessio Augustana' of 1530.

The words of the Confession are these: 'Accessit opinio, quæ auxit privatas missas in infinitum, videlicet quod Christus suâ passione satisfecerit pro peccato originis, et instituerit Missam, in qua fieret oblatio pro quotidianis delictis, mortalibus et venalibus. Hinc manavit publica opinio, quod Missa sit opus delens peccata vivorum et mortuorum ex opere operato.'

And it is important and instructive to mark how this language was received. And here we may fitly make a quotation from Bossuet. He says: 'It is not a matter of surprise that the Catholics, as the Lutherans themselves relate, on hearing this reproach, all, as if with one common voice, cried out against it, saying, "That never had such a thing been heard among them." But the people were to be made believe that these wretched Catholics were even ignorant of the first elements of Christianity.' ('Hist. of Variations,' English trans., vol. i., pp. 134, 135. Dublin, 1845.)

I know not on what Lutheran authority Bossuet has made this statement. There is no mention of any such clamorous interruption in the histories of Seckendorf or of Cœlestinus. And I have failed to find any notice of it in the 'Historia Augustanæ Confessionis' of D. Chytræus. There is no reason, however, to question the fact.

But whatever may have been the outburst of feeling at the time that the Confession was read in the assembly, it concerns us more to inquire how the statement was dealt with in the brief reply drawn up by Arnoldus Wesaliensis and Joannes Cochlæus ('primi nominis inter Pontificios tunc temporis Theologi') with the view of elucidating the true points of the controversy with the Protestants.

This is their answer : 'Quod aiunt, missas in infinitum auctas ex ea opinione, quod Christus sua passione satisfecerit pro peccato originis, instituerit autem missam pro cæteris peccatis abolendis. Nobis profecto verisimile non est, eam opinionem ullius esse Doctoris Catholici, tantum abest, ut apud nos vulgata sit ea opinio. Scimus enim Christum dixisse, hoc facite in meam commemorationem.' (Brevis . . . responsio, De Missa, § 6. In Cœlestinus, 'Hist. Comitiorum, M.D.XXX.,' tom. ii., fol. 237*b*. Francfort-on-Oder, 1597.)

They then go on to affirm just that doctrine concerning the Mass which our Article condemns.

Witness the following: 'Cæterum opinio publica, affirmans missam vivis et mortuis prodesse ex opere operato, improbari non debet' (§ 7). 'In missis est una eademque per commemorationem oblatio, quæ a Christo in cruce semel peracta est. Quod igitur in cruce semel peractum est, in sacrificio missæ sæpe per mysterium repetitur' (§ 9). 'Quod arguunt, per missam non deleri peccata vivorum et mortuorum, eo quod per fidem fiat justificatio. Non magnopere ad negotium facit. Quandoquidem non tam culpa quam pœna peccatis debita per missam deletur, tanquam per bonum opus, quod in se ex opere operato Deo semper gratissimum est' (§ 10).

Let it be well observed that these eminent

Romish Divines, while utterly repudiating the doctrine which, it is alleged, is that condemned by our Article, express the doctrine of the Mass as approved by them in language which might have suggested the very words which our Article uses to describe the doctrine it means to condemn.

But this is not all. Far more important evidence remains. On August 3 there was recited before the Diet (in its abbreviated and castigated form) the Confutation of the Protestant Confession drawn up at the direction of the Emperor by a Committee of Divines,[1] among whom were some of the ablest champions of the Papal cause.

[1] There is a want of agreement as to the actual authors of the 'Confutatio.' A complete list of the Romish Doctors will be found in Cœlestinus, tom. iv., fol. 134*b*.

Seckendorf says that the Theologians ' magno numero consederunt, et intra sex fere hebdomadum tempus, Confutationem, quam vocant, conscripserunt' (Com., Lib. II., sect. 29, § lxvi., p. 171). Mosheim attributes it to Faber, assisted by Eck and Cochlæus (Cent. XVI., sect. 1, ch. iii., vol. iv., p. 140. Edit. Soames). And Hospinian makes special mention of the same three names, putting Eck first (' Hist. Sacr.' Par. II., Op., tom. iv., p. 161), but adding five others (p. 160) as *præcipui* among the Romish Divines, to whom the task of drawing it was committed. Du Pin mentions Faber, Eckius, Conradus de Wimpina, Conradus Collinus, and Cochlæus (' Eccles. Hist.,' Cent. XVI., Book II., ch. xxii., p. 117. Eng. trans., London, 1703).

In this confutation we read: 'Privatarum Missaram abrogatio admitti ac tolerari non potest, neque satis intelligi potest, quod assumitur, Christum satisfecisse suâ passione pro peccato originali, et instituerit Missam pro actuali peccato. Nam hoc numquam auditum est a Catholicis. Jamque rogati plerique, constantissime negant, ab iis sic doceri, non enim Missa delet peccata ... sed delet pœnam pro peccato debitam, satisfactiones supplet, et gratiæ confert augmentum.' (Cœlestinus, tom. iii., fol. 11*b*.)

The confutation goes on to reject the teaching that there is not an offering of Christ in the Mass, and that the oblation is not made for the quick and the dead (fols. 11*b*, 12*a*). It insists that Christ is offered in the Mass, 'ut hostia pacifica' (fol. 12*b*).

But further, after this repudiation of the abuse which had been severely censured by the Confession as first read before the Princes at Augsburg, another edition of the Confession,[1] very carefully amended by Melancthon, was put forth in the year 1540.[2]

---

[1] Various editions, with less important changes, had been published previously; but the changes of 1540 were observable, and caused much controversy.

[2] The 'Confessio invariata' still holds its place in the 'Libri Symbolici' of the Lutheran Church. The 'variata' finds more favour among the Reformed. Its doctrine of the

And how does this 'Confessio variata' deal with the matter of this abuse? It simply omits all reference to it. It deals with the doctrine of the sacrifice as acknowledged by these Romish Divines, and with certain adherent abuses, but it no longer concerns itself with the superstition[1] which these Divines had so distinctly separated from their belief, and which they accused the Protestants of unjustly setting down to their

---

Eucharist is less distinctly Lutheran, and was therefore very displeasing to the sterner Lutherans.

In the matter of the Mass the 'variata' has a closer verbal correspondence with our Article XXXI. Both it and the 'invariata' agree with one another, and with our Article, in insisting on the Sacrifice of the Cross being a propitiation for all sins, both original and actual (Syll. Conf., 140, 194). Both also agree with our Article in making the condemnation of the Mass a necessary consequence of the one propitiation of the Cross. (*Ibid.*, 139, 140, 193, 194.) The following from the 'variata' may well be compared with the language of our Article: 'Si considerabitur, quam late vagatus sit hic error in Ecclesia, quomodo hac persuasione créverit missarum numerus, quomodo vivis et mortuis hoc sacrificio promissa sit remissio culpæ et pœnæ, apparebit ecclesiam propter hanc prophanationem, horrendis peccatis deformatam esse.' (*Ibid.*, 195.)

[1] It should be specially observed that in the 'Confessio invariata' this error of Aquinas is set down as the fruitful source of the multiplication of Masses, as also in Melancthon's 'De Missâ judicium' (Cœlestinus, tom. i., fol. 278*b*). In the 'invariata' there remains the charge of the multiplication of Masses, but this evil is traced to other sources.

account as a Catholic opinion. And this is all the more to be observed, because in his 'Apologia' Melancthon had, indirectly, but very forcibly, vindicated the language of the earlier Confession from the charge of assailing a notion which was an unheard-of imagination, and could hardly have derived support from the language of any reputable doctor.[1]

It should be added that the same observation applies to the 'Confession of Saxony,' written by Melancthon in 1551, to be presented at the Tridentine Council, and which has been regarded as a repetition of the Confession of Augsburg.

In all three of these forms of Lutheran confession is found the same complaint of the extravagant multiplication of Masses. But whereas

[1] His words are : ' Ostendimus rationem, quare missa non justificet ex opere operato, nec applicata pro aliis mereatur eis remissionem. . . . Quare repudiandus est error Thomæ, qui scripsit Corpus Domini semel oblatum in cruce, pro debito originali, jugiter offerri pro quotidianis delictis in altari, ut habeat in hoc Ecclesia munus ad placandum sibi Deum.' ('Libri Symb.,' p. 265. Leipsiæ, 1654.)

So the Lutheran 'orators' sent to the King of England in 1538, in their letter to Henry VIII., thus wrote : 'An potest etiam majis impium quidquam dici, quam illi de Missis istis docuerunt? Nempe quod Christus suâ passione satisfecerit pro peccatis originis, et instituerit Missam, in quâ fieret oblatio pro quotidianis delictis mortalibus et venialibus.' (In Burnet's 'Hist. of Reform.,' Records, Addenda, No. VII., vol. ii., p. cxl. London, 1850.)

in the first (the 'invariata') this evil is set down to the prevalence of the opinion commonly attributed to Aquinas, in the second (the 'variata') it is charged to a false persuasion of the Mass as meriting remission culpæ et pœnæ ('Sylloge Confess.,' p. 193), and in the third (the 'Saxonica') the cause is traced to this—'Multi ante hoc tempus scripserunt, fieri oblationem in Missa pro vivis et mortuis, et mereri eam facienti et aliis remissionem peccatorum ex opere operato' (*Ibid.*, p. 283).

It will hardly be making too much of this to infer that the wiser Protestants were thinking it best to cease attacking a position which was not defended by their opponents. The preliminary skirmishes had tended to clear the atmosphere of mists and mistakes, and to make the true *status controversiæ* stand out more clearly and distinctly.

We may, indeed, very well admit a certain tendency among the Romanists to charge the Protestants with bringing against them false accusations, and to make small allowance for what there may have been to warrant such misunderstandings. But we seem called upon here to give the Lutherans credit for desisting from a charge, the truth of which the Papists had so strongly and indignantly denied. Is there not that which is full of instruction for us here? Are we to suppose it very likely that, after this, the English Reformers would have framed an Article for the very purpose of striking down this repudiated opinion, and that in language which so entirely failed to describe it?

True it is that our Bishop Jewel appeals to the language of Aquinas, and alleges a passage from Catharinus which seems to inculcate the repudiated doctrine. But this he does in answer to the charge of Harding, that in his 'Apology' he had misrepresented Romish doctrine when he affirmed, 'They say . . . that they are able by their Masses to distribute and apply unto men's commodity all the merits of Christ's death; yea, although many times the parties think nothing of the matter, and understand full little what is done.' Harding asks in reply, 'Who ever taught this doctrine in the Catholic Church?' Jewel meets the charge by quotations showing the extent to which the abuses of the Mass had been carried. He does not claim for this abuse that it was then recognised as the Teaching of the Church of Rome, but he alleges that 'this doctrine, *not long sithence*, was holden for Catholic, and was strongly maintained by your Catholic doctors.' He adds, after making the quotation from Catharinus, 'Hereby, M. Harding, ye may see that this doctrine lacketh no defence amongst your Catholics.' (Jewel's Works, P.S. Edit., 'Apology and Defence,' pp. 556-558.)

No one who has any acquaintance with the writings of Bishop Jewel can doubt for a moment that not only the abuses, but the very doctrine of the Mass itself, came under his strong condemnation. What he regarded as the blasphemy of Catharinus was, in his view, the fruit gone to seed of the true Teaching of Rome. The Mass was that which he was aiming at. It was, in his view, a dishonour to the doctrine of the Cross, and the truth of the Gospel. Thus he wrote, ' Touching the use and order of the holy mysteries, Christ saith not, Do this for the remission of your sins; but " Do this in My Remembrance." The only and everlasting sacrifice for sin is the Son of God crucified upon the Cross. . . . Whatsoever doctrine is contrary to this doctrine is wicked and blasphemous, and . . . injurious to the glory and Cross of Christ.' ('Harding, Thess.,' etc., p. 757. P.S. Edit.)

Indeed, all evidence tends to show that at the period of the Reformation whatever hold the opinion attributed to Aquinas may still have had on popular ignorance, it had ceased to have (if it ever had) any appreciable support from Theologians of repute, and that the imputation of any such notion was regarded as an insult to the educated mind of Christendom, as implying an inconceivable ignorance of the first principles of the Christian faith.

That this was the true state of the case can scarcely be doubted. It may be further established by reference to the writings of the celebrated Romish Divine, Albertus Pighius.[1] His fame was not unknown in England. Cranmer knew enough of his writings to detect that Gardener had learned much of his divinity from their study. ('Lord's Supper,' P.S. Edit. p. 127). Bishop Jewel also was familiar with his works, which are frequently referred to by our English Reformers. And Pighius (who died in 1543) had written a treatise, 'De Missæ Sacrificio,' in which he had charged the Protestants with grossly misrepresenting the opinions of their opponents in this very particular.[2] Thus he wrote: 'Qui et hoc admonendi sunt, non se candide egisse, aut agere, qui in

[1] Albertus Pighius obtained some fame as a mathematician and astronomer, but his theological treatises were best known. His opinions on some points were peculiar. He rejected the views of St. Augustin and Aquinas on grace, and on original sin he held much the same doctrine as Catharinus. (See Du Pin, 'Eccles. Hist.,' 16th Cent., p. 437. London, 1703.)

[2] See Appendix, Note F.

suâ confessione, opinionem nobis affingunt, quæ privatas missas in infinitum auxerit. Quod videlicet Christus, suâ passione satisfecerit tantum pro peccato originis, et instituerit missam, in quâ fieret oblatio, pro quotidianis delictis mortalibus et venialibus. Ego sane, qui etiam in Scholis plerisque annis versatus sum, ubi magna est de quovis disputandi quidvis disputationis gratia, et veritatis certius excutiendæ, asserendi licentia, nunquam tamen audivi, nunquam legi, a quopiam proferri opinionem ejusmodi, priusquam eorum confessionem legerem. Nec puto ullum proferre poterunt, seu Scholasticum, seu alium, qui ejusmodi opinionem astruat : et si quem invenissent, non candide facerent, quod unius stoliditatem, nobis omnibus affingerent, qui nihil tale apud nostros, aut legimus, aut audivimas ; et ejusmodi portentis, nostram doctrinam conspergant, commaculent, et traducant, apud harum rerum ignarum, et sibi credulum populum.' ('Contro. Ratisb.,' fol. 116b.)

In the margin we read, 'Quæ nobis palam affingant, a nostra sententia alienissima.'

So Gaspar Contarini (in view of a charge less distinctly defined and less monstrous in form) had spoken indignantly of 'nefanda illa [doctrina] quam nobis inpingunt, nos, scilicet, profiteri Missam, opus, scilicet, illud sacerdotis esse sacrificium, quod[1] æmuletur passionem Christi, per quod novum sacrificium sacerdos nobis mereatur remissionem peccatorum.' And then he asks, 'Quis hoc dicit? Quis hoc sentit; nullus profecto sanæ mentis.' ('De Sacramentis,' lib. ii., Op., p. 360. Paris, 1571.)

This is all the more remarkable an utterance as coming from one who had sympathy with Evangelical doctrine, and was very sensible of the need of Reformation.

Is it credible that our English Theologians, with Cranmer at their head, were concerning themselves to frame an Article on purpose to discredit a monstrous notion which had been denounced as nothing but a vulgar error of the grossest kind by leading Divines of the Romish Church?

---

[1] In writing this Contarini may have had in view the following characteristic words of Luther in the Smalcaldic Articles: 'Campegius Augustæ dixit, se prius omnia tormenta, membrorum dilaniationem et mortem passurum, quam Missam missam facturum esse. Et ego etiam, per Dei opem in cineres corpus meum redigi et concremari patiar prius, quam ut Missarium ventrem, vel bonum vel malum, *æquiparari Christo Jesu*, Domino et Servatori meo, aut eo superiorem esse feram.' (In 'Concordia,' p. 307. Lips., 1654.)

A compendious view of Contarini's own doctrine of the Mass-sacrifice will be found in his 'Christiana Instructio' (Op., pp. 536, 537. Paris, 1571.) While falling far short of the doctrine of Trent, it is by no means clear of mediæval errors.

But the truth may be further confirmed by observing that when, a while later, Bellarmine addresses himself to a confutation of the Augsburg Confession, as reprinted in the Lutheran 'Liber Concordiæ,' he does not fail to take notice of the imputation of this strange teaching in the Romish Church. And how does he notice it? He denounces it as an impudent lie. He says, 'Impudenti mendacio tribuitur Catholicis doctoribus illa divisio, quod Christus passione sua satisficerit solum pro peccato originis, pro actualibus autem institueret Missam. Nemo enim Catholicorum unquam sic docuit; sed credimus et profitemur Christum in cruce pro omnibus omnino peccatis satisfecisse, tam originalibus, quam actualibus; quia tamen meritum passionis Ejus non prodest, nisi certa aliqua ratione applicatur (. . . neque vero sola fide applicari potest . . .). Propterea docet Ecclesia Catholica, ad peccata expianda, sive ad meritum passionis Christi hominibus applicandum, instituta esse varia sacramenta, et ipsum etiam Corporis Domini sacrificium, quæ omnia ex opere operato utilia sint.' ('Judic. de Lib. Concor.,' Mendac. xviii. Op., tom. vii., col. 604. Colon, 1617.)

Did Bellarmine, did any other Romish Divine, ever write thus of our English Article XXXI.? Did any ever accuse the English Church of thus laying to their charge things which they knew not, a doctrine which they rejected?

And, further, when our own Hooker had it laid to his charge by Travers, in his 'Supplication,' that he had made too little of the error of Rome in stating that the Romanists 'teach Christ's righteousness to be the only meritorious cause of taking away sin,' whereas Thomas Aquinas and Archbishop Catharinus teach, 'That Christ took away only original sin, and that the rest are to be taken away by ourselves' (Hooker's 'Works,' vol. iii., p. 563. Edit. Keble), how did Hooker meet this accusation? He quotes Andradius, confessing 'only the merits of Christ open the entering into blessedness.' He quotes Soto, saying, 'It is put for a ground that all, since the fall of Adam, obtain salvation only by the Passion of Christ.' He quotes the Council of Trent, declaring (of the causes of our first justification), 'no meritorious but Christ.' And then he adds, 'Whom to have merited the taking away of no sin but original is not their opinion, which [Travers] himself will find, when he hath well examined his witnesses, Catharinus and Thomas.[1] Their Jesuits (he adds) are marvellously angry with the men out of whose gleanings Mr. Travers seemeth to have taken

[1] See Appendix, Note G.

this; they openly disclaim it; they say plainly, " Of the Catholics there is no one that did ever so teach "; they make solemn protestation, " We believe and profess that Christ upon the Cross hath altogether satisfied for all sins, as well original as actual." ' (Answer to Travers, § 14, in Hooker's ' Works,' vol. iii., pp. 583, 584. Edit. Keble.)

Acknowledging, then, the existence in the dark ages of the gross popular abuse which was not unnaturally connected with the name of Aquinas, and which probably found its patrons chiefly among the monks,[1] and which in more

[1] So it was regarded by Bullinger, as appears from the following : ' Sequuti sunt qui dixere Corpus Christi semel oblatum esse in cruce pro originali peccato, nunc vero offerri jugiter in altari pro delictis nostris quotidianis, adeoque munus hoc datum esse Ecclesiis ad placandam indignationem Dei. . . . Quæ quidem manifesta impietas tanto majores acquisevit vires quanto plures exortæ sunt monachorum sectæ.' (' De Origine Erroris,' fol. 225. Tiguri, 1539.)

Indeed, abuses of the Mass generally seem to have been commonly set down to the account of the monks. Witness the following : 'Repudiandi sunt et reliqui communes errores, quod Missa conferat gratiam ex opere operato facienti. Item, quod applicata pio aliis, etiam injustis non ponentibus obicem, mereatur eis remissionem peccatorum, culpæ et pœnæ. Hæc omnia falsa et impia sunt, nuper ab indoctis Monachis conficta, et obruunt gloriam passionis Christi et justitiam fidei.' (' Apologia pro. Conf. A.' in the ' Concordia,' pp. 265, 266. Lipsiæ, 1654.)

' Aperte damnamus portentosum errorem monachorum,

recent times had seemed to be shielded by a Dominican of extreme and eccentric views, who was finally Archbishop of Conza, we are assuredly justified in affirming that it had not acquired any such general recognition, and had not received any such important support among the doctors of Roman theology, as would warrant the Church of England in framing a separate Article for the express purpose of condemning it.

(*b*) And now, if it be granted that the natural meaning of the Article is a condemnation of the Romish doctrine of the Mass, another historical argument must be added which tells with enormous force against the position of those who would explain away its natural meaning. The forty-two Articles were promulgated in the summer of 1553.[1] We know well what a

---

qui scripserunt, sumptionem mereri remissionem peccatorum, et quidem ex opere operato, sine bono motu utentis.' (Confessio Saxonica, in ' Sylloge Confessionum,' p. 281. Oxford, 1827.)

[1] Certain 'Articles of Religion,' to be subscribed by preachers and lecturers in divinity, appear to have been drawn up by Cranmer as early as February, 1549. (See Hardwick, 'Hist. of Art.,' p. 73.) In the summer of 1551 the King and Privy Council directed 'the Archbishop to frame a book of Articles of Religion, for the preserving and maintaining peace and unity of doctrine in this Church, that, being finished, they might be set forth by public authority.' Before their publication they were submitted to

change soon followed in the history of the English Church. Among the martyrs for the truth in the following reign were some who had had to do with the framing or approving these Articles. Take the case of Ridley and Latimer. They were condemned not only for the denial of transubstantiation, but also for the denial of a certain doctrine concerning the Mass. Will anyone believe that they were put to death for denying such a gross superstition as was repudiated by

---

the other English prelates, and remained with them till the spring of 1552. Then they were forwarded to the Council, and 'soon afterwards appear to have returned to the Archbishop, in whose hands they remained until September 19.' Then the Archbishop ' digested them very carefully,' adding titles and some supplementary clauses. Then a copy was sent to Sir Wm. Cecil and Sir John Cheke for 'their opinion and revision.' Then they were submitted to the King himself. And in the following October the six royal chaplains were directed to consider them. At this stage they were forty-five in number, and entitled 'Articles Concerning an Uniformity in Religion.' Once more they were submitted to Cranmer's scrutiny, and then, after the 'last corrections of his judgment and pen,' returned to the Council, November 24, 1552. On June 19, 1553, the mandate was issued for their subscription. But a fortnight or three weeks previously they had been in circulation, having been published by Grafton in May, as 'agreed on by the bishops and other learned and godly men in the last Convocation.' There is reason to suppose that the amount of alteration resulting from the protracted criticism had been considerable. (See Hardwick, 'Hist. of Art.,' p. 77.)

Romish Divines almost without an exception? Will anyone seriously contend that they were burnt for denying what Melchior Canus has stigmatized as 'Ambrosii Catharini deliratio,' viz., 'peccata ante baptismam admissa per crucis sacrificium remitti, post baptismam vero omnia per sacrificium altaris'? ('De Loc. usu,' Lib. XII., cap. xii., Op., p. 429. Petavii, 1734.) But the process under which they suffered defines the doctrine they denied in terms which make it in substance identical with the doctrine our Article denies. We find in the 'Articles, jointly and severally ministered to Dr. Ridley and Master Latimer, by the Pope's deputy,' as follows: 'Tibi objicimus, quod . . . tu asseruisti, affirmasti, ac palam, publice, et pertinaciter defendisti, in missa non esse vivicum ecclesiæ sacrificium pro salute vivorum et mortuorum propitiabile.' (See Ridley's 'Works,' P.S. Edit., pp. 486, 487.)

This Article was recited to Ridley, and a direct answer required, to which Ridley said, 'Christ, as St. Paul writeth, made one perfect sacrifice for the sins of the whole world; neither can any man reiterate that sacrifice of His, and yet is the communion an acceptable sacrifice to God of praise and thanksgiving. But to say that thereby sins are taken away (which wholly and perfectly was done by Christ's passion, of which the communion is only a memory), that is a great derogation of the merits of Christ's passion; for the sacrament was instituted that we, receiving it, and thereby recognising and remembering His passion, should be partakers of the merits of the same. For otherwise doth this sacrament take upon it the office of Christ's passion, whereby it might follow that Christ died in vain.' (*Ibid.*, p. 275. See also his answer in pp. 206, *sqq.*, and his conference with Latimer, p. 107.)

It must not be hastily assumed that in speaking thus Ridley was showing that he misunderstood or misrepresented the views of his opponents. When he said, 'Whereby it might follow that Christ died in vain,' he was, in truth, but echoing words which had been heard in the Council of Trent. There we are told of one of the Fathers (and he was very far indeed from standing alone in his opinion), 'quoad doctrinam improbavit, quod dicitur Christum in Cœnâ obtulisse seipsum, quia *alias gratis mortuus esset,* quia illud suffecisset ad reconciliandum nos Deo.' (Theiner, 'Acta Conc. Trid.,' tom. i., p. 640.)

Ridley was only standing firm on the Scriptural truth (Heb. ix. 25-28) which the Reformation strongly insisted on, viz., that the Christian faith not only knew only one Propitiatory Sacrifice, but also recognised one only offering of that Sacrifice—an offering or oblation, of the essence of which was the real suffering and death of the Son of God.

Our Reformers, through God's grace, saw clearly and maintained stedfastly, not only the 'one' but the '*once*' of Christ's sacrifice for sins. As against a strong host of objectors, and a whole armoury of superstitious errors, they lifted on high the truth that the Propitiatory Sacrifice of the Christian Church was the Sacrifice indeed of one only Victim; but that, besides and beyond this, it admitted of being once only, because once for all, offered; and that, therefore, every notion of an iterated or continued oblation was as good as a denial of the perfection and completeness of that which had gone before.

Romanists were ever ready to meet the argument from the 'one,' by alleging that what they offered was always *the same*.[1] But for the

[1] So Albertus Magnus, in view of the objection—'In Sacramento nulli facienda est injuria : sed Christus semel oblatus, hominum peccata tulit sufficienter, prout dicit Apostolus : ergo injuria fit ei si totâ die offertur pro peccatis'—answers thus : 'Dicendum quod non fit injuria : quia eadem res semper offertur, et sub uno effectu : sed si quæreretur alia res ad occisionem et redemptionem, tunc

'once' they could but plead that the offering in the Mass is in a different manner of offering— *i.e.*, without real blood-shedding. This new manner contained an *immolatio*[1] (explained as a setting of the Sacrifice on the altar) without an *occisio*. This seemed the only way of evading the force of the ἅπαξ προσενεχθεὶς (Heb. ix. 28). But the answer was obvious. Holy Scripture knows nothing of any variety in the manner of offering. The true view of the 'one' and the 'once' leaves no room for any reiteration in any manner whatever.

It is important to mark that this was one of the strong positions on which our Reformers concentrated their strength. This they felt was to be defended at whatever cost. And this also was that which their opponents were constantly assailing. A few examples will suffice :

---

morti Christi fieret injuria.' (In Lib. IV., Sent. Dist. XIII., Op., tom. xvi., p. 209. Lugd., 1651.)

The Fathers of the Council of Trent mostly followed one another in repeating the same argument as with one mouth.

[1] So it had been taught by Albertus Magnus : 'Dicendum, quod immolatio nostra non tantum est representatio, sed immolatio vera, id est, rei immolatæ oblatio per manus sacerdotum . . . immolatio proprie est oblatio occisi ad cultum Dei: et quoad oblationem non est representatio tantum, sed verus actus offerendi. Sic autem non est de occisione et crucifixione.' (In Lib. IV., Sent. Dist. XIII., Art. xxiii., Op., tom. xvi., p. 209. Lugd., 1651.)

So Philpot was charged with this—'That you have blasphemously spoken against the Sacrifice of the Mass, calling it idolatry and abomination' ('Exam. and Writings,' P.S. Edit., p. 150). To which he replied: 'Your Sacrifice daily reiterated is a blasphemy against Christ's death' (p. 152).

Compare the following from Cranmer's answer to the three Articles given him by the Committee at Oxford: 'Ubi enim peccatorum remissio est, jam non est amplius oblatio pro peccato: propter hoc Christi sacrificium quisquis aliud quæsierit pro pecatis, sacrificium propitians, invalidum et inefficax efficit Christi sacrificium: si enim hoc ad remittenda peccata sufficiens est, alio non est opus. Alterius enim necessitas hujus arguit infirmitatem ac insufficientiam.' (In Collier's 'Eccles. Hist.,' vol. ix., p. 305. Records, No. LXXI.)

Bradford sets this down as second among the 'four special Articles,' that the Papists 'chiefly persecute for.' 'They teach that, though our Saviour Himself did indeed make a full and perfect sacrifice, propitiatory and satisfactory for the sins of all the whole world, never more so, that is to say bloodily, to be offered again, yet in His supper He offered the same sacrifice unto His Father, but unbloodily, that is to say in will and desire; which is accounted often even for the deed as this was. Which unbloody sacrifice He commanded His Church to offer in remembrance of His bloody sacrifice, as the principal mean whereby His bloody sacrifice is applied both to the quick and dead.' ('Letters,' etc., P.S. Edit., p. 270.)

Let it be well noted that this is part of a 'Confutation,' published abroad, it would seem, by the Protestant exiles during the reign of Mary (see p. 267). It is surely impossible to regard this statement of the Mass-doctrine as an unfair representation or an over-statement of Romish teaching. Yet it is for the denial of *this* that the Reformers were persecuted. For the 'Confutation,' see p. 289. Bradford says (p. 285): 'Seeing they reiterate it by this,' they ... are 'dissemblers and destroyers of Christ's sacrifice' (see also p. 317).

Much more might be added. But it is needless to multiply examples. Can we fail to see that our Reformers were condemned to the stake, by the authority of the Pope, for denying just what our Article denies, and for teaching just what our Article teaches?[1] And is it, then,

---

[1] Alluding to the argument of 'the Kiss of Peace,' which would make an identity of doctrine between the words of Ridley and those of the Council of Trent, a learned Roman

possible for us to believe that the Article was intended to teach what Rome teaches, and to deny only what Rome also denied, and to condemn only what Rome would agree to be an abuse to be condemned?

It may indeed very well be allowed that our English Reformers were very sensible of abuses which had become, perhaps, almost identified in men's minds with the notion of the Mass-sacrifice. They saw the tree as it then stood with its leaves and fruit hanging on its branches—leaves and fruit which were not for the healing of the nations, but for the deceiving and turning aside of men's souls. And they aimed, not at plucking off the noxious leaves and poisonous fruit (the Church of Rome and the Council of Trent could aim at such work), but at uprooting the very tree itself on which these grievous superstitions grew, and which was itself a super-

---

Catholic divine wrote with unanswerable force: 'Let us see what this comes to. It is no less than this: that the Reformers were condemned for professing the true Catholic faith as defined by the Council of Trent; that the Catholic doctors, acting under the commission of the Cardinal Legate, who had himself sat as one of the Legates in the Council of Trent, maintained a gross error contrary to the decrees of the Council . . . and that the only persons in this country who now profess the faith for which the Reformers died, besides the author himself, are the Roman Catholics.' (Canon Estcourt, 'Dogmatic Teaching,' p. 62.)

stitious abuse of the institution of Christ. It was the same doctrine which the Church of Rome was upholding, and the Church of England was denying.[1] This Article was as the standard lifted up by the Church of England. The fiercest of the war raged around it. Here was the battle-field on which Rome lit her fires, and English martyrs laid down their lives.

And are we now to be taught that all this was only an unhappy mistake, that Rome was in error in supposing we had aimed anything at her teaching, or that we were in error in supposing Rome's doctrine was opposed to our own ?

These are questions to which surely the thoughts of English Churchmen should now be very seriously directed.

It is surely impossible for those who know the ground which our Reformers defended, and who have it in their hearts to stand where they stood, to hesitate on this matter.

It must be proclaimed aloud that we may not, dare not, cannot go over from the side which pronounced the Sacrifices of Masses to be blasphemous fables, to the side of those whose desire

---

[1] Compare the *Articuli Cleri* of 1558, No. 3. 'Quod in Missa offertur verum Christi Corpus, et verus Ejus Sanguis, sacrificium propitiatorium pro vivis et defunctis.' (Cardwell's 'Synodalia,' p. 493.) See Hook's 'Lives,' New Series, vol. ii., pp. 336, 337.

it seems to be to bring back again these dangerous deceits.

But there is another consideration which must by no means be omitted. The arguments, indeed, from an *animus* supposed in some few Liturgical changes may easily be overstrained. But the doctrinal character imparted to our Book of Common Prayer by excisions, and transpositions, by additions, and alterations—all indicating clearly a consistent and persistent design—can never, in fairness, be ignored. The argument derived from this character, when added to the cumulative evidence derived from other sources, is of very great weight indeed. And that weight is greatly enhanced by the light thrown upon the changes in the controversy between Gardiner and Cranmer. This argument has scarcely yet been weighed at its true value. Rather its force has been very imperfectly estimated. Here it must suffice to touch upon the matter in the most cursory manner. We take but the broad fact which must be acknowledged of all. A revision of the Liturgy may be said to have been contemporary with the framing of our Forty-two Articles.[1]

---

[1] The Revised Book of Common Prayer was published in 1552 (Cranmer and his coadjutors having been engaged upon it since the autumn of 1550), and was ordered to be

That revision was declared to be for the purpose of making our Prayer-Book 'fully perfect.'[1] It is impossible to question the design of its corrections. With a carefulness which, if erring, erred in the way of excess of caution, it pruned away whatever sounded of a sacrificial sense that could be at all assimilated to the Mass-doctrine of Rome. Ambiguities which might have been supposed to offer shelter for a corporal Presence on the altar were diligently cast away. Whatever could be supposed (even in error) to lend any sort of support to the idea of a sacrificial memorial or oblation made by the priest on the altar was removed.[2] The altar itself was no more to be found. What did all this mean? It is impossible to suppose that it meant nothing. What did it mean to exclude from the teaching of the English Church? Was it the strange

---

used from the Feast of All Saints. It was confirmed by Parliament in April, and finally came into use November 1, 1552, when Ridley officiated at St. Paul's Cathedral.

[1] See 'Papers on the Doctrine of the English Church,' pp. 512, *sqq.*, specially p. 518.

See also 'Some Recent Teachings concerning the Eucharistic Sacrifice,' pp. 22-25.

A fuller treatment of this subject is yet to be desired.

[2] The Sacrificial language, for the most part, had already been removed in 1549. On the further elimination of 1552 see 'Recent Teachings concerning the Eucharistic Sacrifice,' pp. 15, 16; and 'Papers on the Eucharistic Presence.' pp. 442, *sqq.*

superstition afterwards called by the name of Catharinus? Will anyone dare to contend that *that* was ever in the Roman Missal or in the English Liturgy? The supposition is too absurd to be entertained by anyone for a moment. Then, what sacrificial doctrine could the Revision have meant to exclude but the doctrine of the Romish Mass? The absence of sacrificial language, which some so grievously lament, is the absence of that which has been, not merely declined, but cast away, and cast away, not carelessly, but of set purpose, and clearly of the same set purpose to which we owe such a marked and significant change in our Ordinal,[1] and to which also is to be attributed the unhesitating utterance of our Article.[2]

And, further, this witness of our Prayer-Book stands unshaken still. Nay, it is only strengthened by the fact that efforts were made at the last review to bring back again somewhat of that which had been cast away. These efforts were made, not in the interests of any Romanizing faction, but by men who, thinking there was sufficient witness against Rome in our Articles, were willing to repair what they re-

---

[1] See 'Papers on Doctrine of the English Church,' pp. 533-536.

[2] See Appendix, Note H.

garded as a Liturgical loss by a restoration of what they believed to be capable of a sound and Protestant sense. But even these efforts were all made in vain. The reactionary influences (in relation to the excesses of the Commonwealth) which were then powerfully at work, and the few changes which were then effected, only tend to make this fact more conspicuous and more remarkable. And the history of our own times is surely vindicating the caution of our Reformers and the wisdom of our Revisers.

On this subject let the following wise words be quoted from a divine recently taken from us, to whom the Church of England is deeply indebted : ' The erroneous teaching of the Church of Rome on the subject of the Eucharistic Sacrifice, as it was the occasion, so it is the justification, of the Church of England in excluding from her Communion Service forms of expression which occur in the Ancient Liturgies, but which Rome has perverted to a sense foreign to that in which they are there employed. The same cause has led her to give less prominence to the idea of Sacrifice than confessedly is given to it in those Liturgies, though not less than is given to it in the New Testament. Still, in all essential points she is in accordance with the Church of the first ages. . . . But having had sad experience of the abuse which has grown out of the language freely used in an unsuspecting age, she has been careful, with jealous carefulness, not to let slip from her lips a single expression which might seem to countenance the notion of Sacrifice in a sense for which, as she believes, there is no warrant in Scripture, of which the early Church never dreamt, and which she does not hesitate to characterize, in the strong language of her 31st Art., as a blasphemous fable, and a dangerous deceit.' (Professor Heurtley, 'Sermons on Recent Controversy,' pp. 64, 65.)

But all this, it may be said, is arguing from that which is outside of our Article. It is true. And it should never have been brought in for the purpose of forcibly bending the sense of our Article to signify that which is contrary to, or over and beyond its natural meaning. For any such purpose let it be powerless. But, nevertheless, it may and it ought to come down with overwhelming and crushing power against all attempts to make void the natural sense of the Article by an historical argument which aims at making us believe that it only had in view that which Romanists would abhor as well as ourselves.

It is the natural sense of our Article, and

nothing else, which we are concerned to vindicate. Let its language be fairly expounded, and in the strength of its expressions will be found the index of the true Protestantism of the English Church. Why should the language of our Article be interpreted by a different rule from that of other reformed confessions?

In the 'Westminster Confession of Faith' we have the following: 'In the Sacrament Christ is not offered up to His Father, nor any real Sacrifice made at all, for remission of sin of the quick and dead. . . . So that the Popish Sacrifice of the Mass (as they call it) is most abominably injurious to Christ's one only Sacrifice, the alone propitiation for all the sins of the elect' (ch. xxix.).

It will hardly be contended that this was only a condemnation of the language of Catharinus, or of such like corruptions of the Mass-doctrine. In expression it differs from our Article in pointing to what was then a post-Tridentine dogma, instead of what had been a pre-Tridendite opinion. Beyond this its doctrinal statement cannot fairly be distinguished from that of our Article.

If history is to be appealed to, we have a right to argue that the witness of history gives evidence, not against, but decidedly in favour of, this natural sense. Viewed in the light of its historical surroundings, it may be said that to fancy we see in this Article only an anti-Catharine teaching is much the same thing as to imagine that we see an acorn growing on a fig-tree, or a hawthorn berry on a vine-branch. It would be something strange and startling enough to cause us to question the report of our eyesight, and bid us give to the matter a closer inspection.[1]

---

[1] The *Reformatio Legum Ecclesiasticarum* has no ecclesiastical authority, and in some respects its teaching may fall short of that of our Prayer-Book. But this fact by no means makes void its historical testimony to the views and purposes of our Reformers. It was in process of construction at the same time with our Articles, and was the work of nearly the same hands. 'On this account,' says Hardwick, 'it often forms an excellent commentary on the Articles themselves.' ('Hist. of Art.,' p. 82. See also especially the preface to the 'Reformatio,' pp. x, xi. Oxford, 1550. And Jenkyns's 'Cranmer,' vol. iv., p. 111.)

The following chapter ('De Missis et purgatorio') is an instructive commentary on Article XXXI., and clearly indicates what was in our Reformers' view the error to be opposed in the doctrine of the Mass : 'Quorundam nimis est curiosa perversitas, qui veniam quidem peccatorum expectant, sed hanc morte Christi per solam fidem ad nos accommodatam plene non credunt et omnibus partibus impleri. Quapropter alia requirunt sacrificia, quibus perpurgari possint, et ad hanc rem missas exhibent in quibus sacrificium Deo Patri credunt oblatum esse, nimirum Corpus et Sanguinem Domini Nostri Jesu Christi vere, quomodoque illi dicunt realiter, ad veniam peccatorum

(d) Something might fitly be added—and something of considerable weight—as to the teaching of the Second Book of Homilies.

For, if our Article had been meant to point only to such gross superstitious errors as that of Catharinus, with what consistency could the Church of England have put into the mouths of her ministers such language as the following?

'Neither can he be devout that otherwise doth presume than it was given by the author. We must, then, take heed lest of the memory it be made a sacrifice' (p. 396).

'Now, if we will compare this with the Church of Rome, not as it was in the beginning, but as it is presently, and hath been for the space of nine hundred years and odd, you shall well perceive the state thereof to be so far wide from

---

impetrandam, et salutem tam mortuorum quam vivorum procurandam; quibus etiam regnum tam latum dant ut illis aliquando minui, nonnunquam omnino tolli purgatorii tormenta statuunt. Quâ in re sacrificium illud unicum (quod Christus Dei Filius in Cruce Deo Patri repræsentavit et plenissime exhibuit) largiter imminuunt, et sacerdotium quod unius Christi proprium est, ad miserabilem hominum conditionem devolvunt. Verum sacræ Scripturæ solam Christi mortem nobis ad delictorum purgationem reservant, nec ullum ponunt aliud sacrificium quod ad hanc rem valere possit, imo de purgatorio sane ipsorum ne una quidem syllaba sacris in Scripturis invenitur.' (Cap. x., pp. 12, 13. Oxford, 1850.)

the nature of the true Church, that nothing can be more. . . . Christ commended to His Church a Sacrament of His Body and Blood: they have changed it into a sacrifice for the quick and the dead' (p. 414).

(e) But, before we close our consideration of this subject, we must not omit to notice that there is another side-light from history which may fairly be thrown on the interpretation of our Article. In this light is brought out very clearly, as I think, before our view, the distinct repugnance between this Article and the teaching of the Tridentine Council.

The Article, as we have seen, was of earlier date than the Session of the Council, which determined the doctrine of the Mass. But it was not before the subject had been discussed at Trent.

It was as early as December, 1551, that certain Articles were submitted to the Council for examination and discussion bearing on two subjects, viz., the Sacrifice of the Mass, and the Sacrament of Orders. The Articles were obviously intended to be the expression of the Protestant views with which the Council would have to deal. They are described by Theiner as 'Articuli hæreticorum.' And they are headed thus:

Articuli de sacrificio Missæ et Sacramento ordinis per DD. Theologos examinandi, an sint hæretici et damnandi per S. Synodum.' Among all these Articles there is not one that can be said to refer in the remotest degree to the error attributed to Aquinas. They are expressive of a denial (1) of the offering of Christ in the Mass; (2) of the Sacrifice of Mass availing for the quick and the dead; (3) of its being propitiatory for pain or guilt. And (4) they are expressive of the opinion that the Sacrifice of the Mass is a derogation from the all-sufficiency of the Sacrifice of the Cross. The following brief extracts will suffice to give evidence of this : ' I. Missam non esse sacrificium, nec oblationem pro peccatis.' ' V. Missam nec vivis nec mortuis ut sacrificium prodesse ; et impium esse applicare eam pro peccatis, pro satisfactionibus, et aliis necessitatibus.' ' III. Blasphemiam irrogari sanctissimo Christi sacrificio in cruce peracto, si quis credat Dei Filium denuo in Missa Deo Patri offerri ' (Theiner, vol. i., p. 602). See ' Le Plat, Mon. ad p. Conc. Trid.,' tom. iv., pp. 334, 335.

The discussion which followed in the ' Congregatio Theologorum ' made it quite evident that these opinions would be condemned by the Council. And in January, 1552, certain of the Fathers were deputed by the ' Congregatio Generalis ' ' pro formandis canonibus super articulis de Missa et ordine, et aptanda doctrina jam examinita' (Theiner, tom. i., p. 645). This committee at once proceeded with the work; and on January 18 presented to the Fathers their draft of 'Canones de sacrificio Missæ examinandi per Patres.'[1] Let it suffice to quote from these enough for our present purpose. 'I. Si quis dixerit, in Missa non esse sacrificium, nec oblationem pro peccatis . . . . anathema sit.' 'VII. Si quis dixerit, missam nec vivis, nec mortuis ut sacrificium prodesse; aut impium esse applicare eam pro peccatis, pro satisfactionibus, et aliis necessitatibus: anathema sit.' 'IV. Si quis dixerit, blasphemiam irrogari summo Christi sacrificio in cruce peracto ab iis, qui Dei Filium a sacerdotibus in Missa Deo offerri credunt: anathema sit.'

In those days news did not travel very rapidly from Trent to England.[2] But all ears were open

---

[1] Owing *first* to delay, and *then* to the unexpected suspension of the Council, these decrees and Canons were never formally promulgated. (See Waterworth, pp. 121, 122.)

[2] Of a decree of the Council of Trent, passed October 11, 1551, Cranmer writes 'ut audio' on March 20, 1552.

See also P. Martyr's letter of March 6, 1552, to R. Gualter, in 'Orig. Letters,' P.S., p. 502.

The fifteenth session of the Council was held on January 25, 1552, when a decree was read in which it was stated that matters had been prepared relating to the Sacrifice of the Mass and the Sacrament of order, as well as four to hear what could be heard of the proceedings of the Council. And it is not easy to be believed that no sound of these things—though

Articles on the Eucharist; but that, seeing the Protestants were not come, and an assurance was given that with a more ample safe-conduct they would, the Council 'has deferred the fore-mentioned decrees to the next session of March 19.' (See Mendham, 'Mem. of C. of Trent,' p. 161.)

But though the Protestant theologians were not come, the Saxon and Wittemberg ambassadors were there (p. 160), and would be certain to obtain and disseminate what information they could.

Moreover, six Protestant divines afterwards arrived at Trent. (See Sarpi, p. 352, Brent's translation. London, 1676.)

On November 8, 1551, Dr. Malvenda wrote to the Bishop of Arras: 'I doubt not but your Lordship has had an account of all that passed here, and of the Divines having spoke.' (In Dr. M. Geddes' 'Council of Trent not a Free Assembly,' p. 164. London, 1714.)

Writing on October 12, 1551, he speaks of the wish of the Elector of Cologne that nothing decided upon should be published 'henceforward,' before the end of the Council, but fears 'that the Legate will start such difficulties against it, particularly its not having been the course that has been taken from the beginning of the Council, that it will not be practised.' (*Ibid.*, p. 162.) See also pp. 28, 101, 121, 167.

Any attempts to stay the spread of information were little likely to attain their object.

Of the session of November 25, 1551, we are told: 'The Legate used all diligence that the decrees might not be printed. And his order was observed at Ripa, where the press was, and where the other decrees were printed. But no man could hinder the sending of many copies out of Trent; whereupon they were printed in Germany, and the difficulty and delay to let them see light made the critics it may have been but a vague rumour—had reached the ears of those engaged in drawing up or revising our Forty-two Articles of 1553. But, indeed, it scarcely needed that any account of these proceedings should have arrived in England for our Reformers to be well assured that the Council of Trent would be defending and maintaining, not the exploded superstition of

---

curious and diligent to examine them more exactly to find the cause of this secrecy.' (Sarpi, p. 335.)

The letter of Cranmer to Calvin of March 20, 1552, has an important bearing on the argument in the text as showing the purpose which was in Cranmer's mind, his understanding in relation to the action of the Council, and especially as regards the doctrine of the Eucharist.

It is incredible that the influence of that purpose should not have been felt in the English Synod and in the framing of our Articles. Thus he wrote: 'Adversarii nostri habent nunc Tridenti Sua Consilia, ut errores stabiliant, et nos piam Synodum congregare negligemus, ut errores refutare, dogmata repurgare et propagare possimus? Illi περὶ τῆς ἀρτολατρείας (ut audio) decreta condunt, quare nos omnem lapidem movere debemus, non solum ut alios adversus hanc idololatriam muniamus, sed etiam ut ipsi in doctrina hujus sacramenti Consentiamus.' (In Cranmer's Works, edit. Jenkyns, vol. iv., p. 346. See also 'Orig. Letters,' P.S., i., p. 24.)

So also in a letter to Bullinger of the same date he had expressed a hope that 'in Anglia, aut alibi, doctissimorum et optimorum virorum Synodus convocaretur, in quâ de puritate ecclesiasticæ doctrinæ et præcipue de consensu controversiæ sacramentariæ tractaretur.' (*Ibid.*, p. 345.) And this he desired 'quemadmodum adversarii nostri nunc Tridenti habent sua consilia ad errores confirmandos.'

Catharinus, but the doctrine of the Mass as then commonly received. The lamented death of Gaspar Contarini long before the Council met, the preponderating influence of the Jesuits,[1] the resolute *animus* manifested by the Fathers against concessions to the doctrine of the Reformers[2]— these things left little room for hope or expectation that anything would be done at Trent to limit or restrain or modify the prevailing popular notion, according to which it was commonly said

---

[1] What might perhaps be called the Evangelical party in the Council did indeed make its voice heard. (See Sarpi, tom. i., p. 335 ; also Le Plat, 'Mon.,' tom. vii., Part II., p. 21; and Hardwick's 'Reformation,' p. 309.)

Hardwick says, 'This party was, however, silenced by a large majority; while the leaders of the Reformation movement, who had anxiously observed the course of the proceedings, were horror-struck by the denunciations of their favourite dogma' (p. 309).

[2] Dr. Vargas wrote, January 20, 1552, to the Bishop of Arras : 'It is plain that all they drive at is to get all the Pope's pretensions established, under the doctrines of order, and so, instead of healing, to destroy and ruin all.' (Dr. Geddes' 'Council of Trent not a Free Assembly,' p. 101. London, 1714.)

And again, on February 28, 1552 : 'The Legate's soul is ready to leap out of his body, to have the clauses of the doctrine of order passed and determined; he promotes everything that tends to that end, on purpose to shut the door against the Protestants.' (*Ibid.*, p. 121.)

See on the subject of these letters Burnet's 'Hist. of Reform.,' Part IV., book iv., vol. ii., p. 742, *sqq.* London, 1850.

that the priest did offer Christ for the quick and the dead, to have remission of pain or guilt. At the date of drawing up the Articles of Religion, it was, indeed, scarcely possible for anyone to suppose for a moment that the Tridentine Council would think of upholding what the Protestants regarded as 'the error of Thomas,' and what Romanists could speak of as 'the madness of Catharinus ;' but it was also impossible for our Reformers to doubt that the Council was about to uphold the generally received doctrine of the Propitiatory Sacrifice of the Mass.[1] And just this, and this only it was, which they proceeded to denounce in what was then their 30th Article.

It will probably be allowed that even this much concerning the history of the Council goes some little way towards the elucidation (if elucidation is needed) of the doctrine of our Article. But there is more to be added :

[1] In 1553 a tract was put forth by Vergerio, to which were prefixed the following questions and answers :

'In concilio Tridentino—

'Causa dijudicanda quæ ? *Controversia inter Papistas et Lutheranos.*

'Judices qui ? *Papa cum suis conjuratis Episcopis et Prælatis, seductionis a Lutheranis annos supra 30 accusati.*

'Accusatores qui ? *Iidem qui et judices.*

'Rei qui ? *Lutherani, Papatus accusatores.*

'Damnabuntur qui ? *Nec judices, nec accusatores Lutheranorum, sed Lutherani, accusatores Papistarum.*'

See Mendham, 'Memoirs,' p. 167.

The Council of Trent, when it proceeded to deal with the subject in 1662, was certainly not ignorant of the Articles of the Church of England. And the notice they afterwards took of Bishop Jewel's Apology[1] is evidence (if evidence were needed) that they were certainly far from being unmindful of the religious affairs of this land. We need not, indeed, suppose that in drawing up the Canons of the Council any preeminent regard[2] was had to the progress of heresy in England. But we cannot doubt that the following Canon was aimed at the very doctrine which our Article was teaching. And if

[1] 'It [the Apology of the Church of England] was read and sharply considered in your late covent at Trident, and great threats made there that it should be answered, and the matter by two notable learned bishops taken in hand—the one a Spaniard, the other an Italian; which two, notwithstanding, these five whole years have yet done nothing, nor, I believe, intend anything to do.' (Jewel, 'Apol. Defence,' P.S. Edit., p. 186.)

In 1563, we are told, 'they consulted at Rome and in Trent to proceed against the Queen of England' (Sarpi, lib. viii., p. 679, Brent's translation), but were dissuaded by the Emperor, whose 'admonition was so effectual that the Pope desisted in Rome, and revoked the commission given to the Legates in Trent.' (*Ibid.*, pp. 679, 680.) The action, however, of certain of the divines at Trent in 1562 led the way to *recusancy*. (Mosheim, vol. iii., p. 406.) The *Brutum Fulmen* followed in 1570.

[2] Bishop Cosin, however, considers that the Canons were directed against *our* doctrine. (Works, vol. v., p. 336, A. C. E.)

the framers had had that Article before their eyes they could hardly have fashioned their anathema more distinctly against it: 'Si quis dixerit, Missæ sacrificium tantum esse laudis, et gratiarum actionis, aut nudam commemorationem sacrificii in cruce peracti, non autem propitiatorium; vel solo prodesse sumenti; neque pro vivis et defunctis, pro peccatis, pœnis, satisfactionibus et aliis necessitatibus offerri debere: anathema sit' (Sess. XXII., Can. 3).

But, further, we think it is scarcely possible to doubt that the language of our Article was subsequently altered for the very purpose of bringing it into still more distinct opposition to the language and the teaching of the Tridentine Canons.

For, whereas the 30th Article of 1553 had gone no further than to assert that the sacrifices of Masses were *figmenta* (forged fables), and the Council of Trent, in 1562, had decreed (Sess. XXII., Can. 4), 'Si quis dixerit, BLASPHEMIAM irrogari sanctissimo Christi sacrificio in cruce peracto, per Missæ sacrificium, aut illi per hoc derogari: anathema sit,' the revision of the English Articles in 1562-63[1] (following close upon

---

[1] The twenty-second session of the Council (to which belong the doctrine and Canons concerning the Mass) was celebrated September 17, 1862. (See Waterworth, 'Canons and Decrees,' p. 152.)

this) added the word 'BLASPHEMA' to the Latin copy, making the Article to read thus: '*blasphema figmenta sunt.*'[1]

As yet, however, the English version remained unaltered. Masses were still spoken of only as 'forged fables.' But in the further and last revision of 1571,[2] the English version was also altered to bring it distinctly under the anathema of the Roman Canon, and the words 'forged fables' were made to give way to the expression '*blasphemous*[3] fables.'

The first revision of our Articles was concluded on the 29th of the following January. (See Cardwell's 'Synodalia,' p. 511.)

[1] In order to estimate aright the force of this argument, it should be observed that this change does not stand alone, but is one among others made in 1562 'with an especial eye to the language of the Decrees of Trent, and in opposition to them.' (See Bishop Philpotts in 'Letters to Butler,' p. 321.)

[2] This change is not found in the MS. copy which is in the Library of Corpus C. College, Cambridge. But it is made in the printed copies (of which three editions, I believe, were issued in 1571). Dr. Bennet says of the changes made in 1571: 'It must be considered that the *Latin* Text is the original; and 'tis manifest, that the far greatest part of the English corrections were intended to make the new translation express the original more properly, more intelligibly to an ordinary reader, or otherwise more suitably to the mind of that convocation ... than the old one did.' (Essay on Thirty-nine Articles, p. 312. London, 1715. See also p. 304.)

[3] Blasphemy need not be understood in its fullest sense, as interpreted in the 'Reformatio Legum Ecclesiasticarum'

Now, let there be a calm view taken of the position as it was in the days of Queen Elizabeth, and after the promulgation of the Tridentine decrees.

Will anyone maintain that if our Articles had been framed for the first time when those decrees had been published in England, it would have been possible to question that they were pointed at the doctrine which the Trent Fathers had maintained?

But now we see that our 31st Article was on the anvil again in 1562, and yet again in 1571, after the doctrine of the Mass had been settled in the Council. And if the Article had not been intended to touch the doctrine as there determined, it would have been easy, and it would surely have been a duty, to remodel its statement that it might clearly appear to be condemning no doctrine of Rome.

But what do we see? We see the Article coming afresh from the anvil with only a verbal

---

('De Blasphemia,' cap. i., pp. 28, 29. Oxford, 1850), but in the Scriptural sense of 'an assumption of those attributes which belong to God alone' (see Wordsworth on Rev. xiii. 6, p. 225), or a professing to do what the Son of God has done and finished. It may be well expressed in the words of the 'Reformatio L. E.': 'Sacerdotium quod unius Christi proprium est, ad miserabilem hominum conditionem devolvunt' (p. 13).

change, but a change which tends to bring it into more distinct and obvious antagonism to the Tridentine Canons. With all this before our eyes, we are surely warranted in affirming that if we are to be persuaded that the doctrine signified by our Article is not the doctrine of the Mass, we need other and much stronger evidence than that which shows that behind this doctrine there was a Monkish teaching yet more monstrous, which could utter (for the ignorant populace) great swelling words of vanity still more blasphemous.

English Churchmen need sometimes to be reminded that there are maximizers as well as minimizers in the Church of Rome. Some of us would perhaps be astonished at the wide extent of liberty of opinion which sometimes seems to be allowed within her communion. Among the maximizers, it would seem that even now some teach an abuse of the Romish Mass-doctrine which makes approaches perilously near to that view of the propitiation which Bellarmine stigmatized as not sacrifice but sacrilege. We cannot say whether any of the writings suggestive of this view have been placed upon the Index. One of them has received the *imprimatur* of Cardinal Manning. (See below, p. 123.)

Among the minimizers may be found some

whose Mass-doctrine, so far as its propitiatory efficacy is concerned, seems to be brought down to something more attenuated than the shadow of a shade.[1] Indeed, it is not to be wondered at if Romish divines for the most part are found to be minimizers when they come to deal distinctly with the efficacy of the Sacrifice. Is there not here a necessity laid upon them? How else can they defend their doctrine of Mass-Sacrifice in its propitiatory character from the charge of dishonouring the one propitiation of the Cross? Here comes in a vast variety of opinion among them. And here we see also a drawing towards us in some most controverted points of some eminent Romish doctors, 'albeit,' as Bishop Morton observes, 'as rowers looking backward to their own purposes and conclusions.' ('On Euch.,' Book VI., cap. vi., p. 469.) And here is manifest what seems to be, in the case of some forms of their teaching, grievous inconsistency.[2]

[1] See Appendix, Note I.

[2] It is surely ridiculous to claim for the Mass-sacrifice that it is the same as the Sacrifice of the Cross, differing only in the manner of offering (see Bona, 'De Missâ,' cap. i., § 1), and to rest its efficacy on the words 'shed for the remission of sins,' and to insist on the Real Presence on the altar for the purpose *merendi et satisfaciendi* (see Morton, 'Inst. of Sacr.,' p. 475. London, 1635), and then to reduce its propitiatory character primarily to its power of moving

For is it not an inconsistency indeed[1] to require as of the necessity of the Sacrifice that they must have on the altar the very Body and

---

the heart to repentance that so there may be obtained remission of sin. (See Bona, ' De Missâ,' cap. i., §§ 1 and 3, and cap. iv., § 10.)

On Romish evasions of the sense of propitiation and satisfaction, see Cranmer on Lord's Supper, pp. 361, 362, P.S. Edit.; and Jewel (Harding, 'Thess.'), pp. 752-757; and Morton, ' Inst. of Sacr.,' Book VI., cap. viii.

Dens declares, ' Ecclesia certò habet suos sacerdotes: ergo hi ad Sacrificia pro peccatis offerenda constituti sunt [Heb. v. 1]: jam vero Sacrificium *pro peccatis offerri, et esse propitiatorium*, sunt synonyma.' ('Tract. Theol.,' pp. 368, 369. Dublin, 1812.)

[1] There seems a strange inconsistency in one sacrifice—itself a true, proper, and propitiatory sacrifice—deriving its efficacy from another, of which it is a memorial, and with which it is also identified. The mind is bewildered in its attempt to grasp the idea of the same sacrifice once only offered, and yet repeatedly offered in another form, each repetition being a memorial of the one sacrifice once offered, and yet itself a propitiatory sacrifice.

It was well said by one, himself a convert from the Mass-doctrine : ' Quanta est differentia inter similitudinem rei et rem ipsam, inter commemorationem actionis et actionem, tantum interest inter sacrificium Corporis Christi activum, et sacrificium Ejus commemorativum, id est, inter passionem Christi, et passionis Ejus simulacrum, quod in Eucharistia repræsentatur. Ergo per eandem consequentiæ necessitatem, tantum distat inter symbola Corporis et Sanguinis, id est, panem et vinum, quibus ea sacrificii memoria et similitudo perficitur, et inter Corpus ipsum et Sanguinem, quantum est discrimen sacrificii, quod revera factum est, et ejus quo illius veri recordatio commemoratur. Tam falso

Blood of the Saviour present by the Real Presence of Transubstantiation, that Christ may be, in some sense, sacrificially offered in immolation to the Father, and then to bid us regard the Sacrifice as nothing more than an acted prayer, or as something equivalent to the offering of a supplication in the name and through the merits and mediation of the Sacrifice of Christ?[1]

It is here in this minimized doctrine of Sacrificial efficacy (and even Bellarmine is a minimizer here) that we find room for charitable hope that many in the Romish communion may yet rest their faith on the one perfect Sacrifice of Christ. And it is here also that a handle seems given to those who would fain find a way of reconciliation between the Communion Service of our Church and the Mass-Sacrifice of Rome.[2] A prayer in

---

igitur Pontificii utrumque sacrificium unum idemque esse contendunt, cum alterum sit ἐξιλαστικὸν, alterum ἀναμνηστικὸν, quam falso symbola ipsa quibus celebratur ἀναμνηστικὸν, una esse putant cum corpore et sanguine Christi, qui in cœlo est. Quod quomodo procedere possit nulla ratione unquam ostenderint.' (Simplicius Verinus, alias C. Salmasius, 'De Transubstantiatione Liber,' pp. 47, 48. Hagiopoli, 1646.)

[1] See Appendix, Note J.

[2] Dens defines the difference between prayer and the Mass *quoad effectum* thus: 'Quod oratio non sit impetratoria nisi ex opere operantis; hoc autem Sacrificium sit impetratorium ex opere operato' ('Tract. Theol.,' p. 374. Dublin, 1812), a statement which, however, he immediately qualifies.

act instead of in words! A pleading of the merits of Christ's Sacrifice before God! Put a favourable interpretation on such words, and is there a true son of the Church of England who would wish to see less than this in our Eucharist? But where, then, is the need of an Altar and a Priest, and a 'Christus ex pane factus,' and an immolation of a Real and Proper Sacrifice? Full well did Bishop Andrewes[1] declare in his controversy with Bellarmine, 'Abate us your Transubstantiation, and there will soon be no contention about the Sacrifice. A memorial of the Sacrifice we readily grant, though we can never grant you the sacrifice of your bread-made Christ.'[2]

But did Bellarmine abate this? Will Rome abate this now? Nay; the Real Presence of Transubstantiation, the Real Presence on the Altar of Christ Himself to be offered for the

[1] This saying of Bishop Andrewes, like other similar utterances by English divines, has sometimes been much misunderstood. For a vindication of its true meaning, see Stillingfleet's Works, vol. vi., p. 179. London, 1710. See also 'Romish Mass and English Church,' p. 28.

[2] Let it be well observed that when Bishop Andrewes wrote 'Sacrificari ibi Christum vestrum *de pane factum*, nunquam daturi' ('Ad Bell. Responsio,' p. 251, A. C. L.), he was but echoing the language of Bellarmine himself: 'Non panis, sed id quod *ex pane factum* est, proprie sacrificatur.' 'Corpus Christi non est victima in sacrificio

quick and the dead, is still of the very essence of the Mass-Sacrifice. And the faith of the Romanist is bound up in the Creed of Pope Pius IV.: 'Profiteor ... in missa offerri Deo, verum, proprium et propitiatorium sacrificium, pro vivis et defunctis; atque in sanctissimo eucharistiæ sacramento esse vere, realiter et substantialiter, corpus et sanguinem, una cum anima et divinitate Domini nostri Jesu Christi.'[1]

---

missæ, absolute, sed ut est in specie panis: in specie autem panis plane visibile est.' ('De Missâ,' lib. i., cap. xxvii.; 'De Controv.,' tom. iii., c. 1041. Ingoldt., 1601.) 'Offerimus Corpus Domini in specie panis, et *ex pane confectum.*' (*Ibid.*, c. 1037.)

[1] 'De ratione veri et proprii Sacrificii est, ut Deum, cur offertur, placet reddatque propitium, at ab eo impetret aut veniam peccatorum, aut pœnarum remissionem, aut alia bona.' (Perrone, 'Prælect. Theol.,' vol. iii., p. 236.)

Professor Mozley has well said: 'Why, then, did the Fathers of Trent, when they had all human language at their command, deliberately choose to call the Sacrifice of the Mass *vere propitiatorium* ? They may have said that it was *vere propitiatorium* in the secondary sense; but no one can fail to see the misleading effect of such language, and that nothing could have been easier to the divines of Trent, had they chosen, than to draw a far more clear distinction than they did between the Sacrifice of the Mass and the Sacrifice of the Cross. It is evident that as ecclesiastical statesmen they were afraid of interfering with the broad, popular, established view of the Mass, while as theologians they just contrived to secure themselves from the responsibility of a monstrous dogmatic statement.' (Lectures, etc., p. 217.)

If it be so that the priest does indeed offer Christ (present with the Real Objective Presence of His Body and Blood) for the quick and the dead, and if this offering has indeed relation to the remission of sins as the relation (in some sort) of cause and effect, if the faith of the Christian is to look to the oblation of the Mass-priest as, in any sense, doing the work of releasing from *pœna* or *culpa*, and if the Priest by his work does indeed do this, then it makes no very material difference (as regards one important aspect of the character of the offering) whether the efficacy be drawn independently from the Sacrifice of the Mass, or derivatively from the satisfaction of the Cross. In the one case, indeed, there is a more gross and grievous superstition, because there is a more direct contradiction of a fundamental Article of the Christian faith. But in the other case there is not a less real derogation from the All-sufficiency of the Oblation of Christ; and, consequently, the Sacrifices of Masses are not a whit less truly blasphemous fables and dangerous deceits. This character does not belong to Masses, because of their being sacrifices absolute in themselves, and efficacious apart from the Sacrifice of the Cross—the Article does not charge them with this—but because of their professing to be efficacious additions to the one perfect Oblation once for all made.

The charge against the Mass-priest is simply that of pretending to do (in a different manner) what Christ did, and consummated by doing. It is no answer to say that Christ is the true Priest who offers by the hand of the earthly minister.[1] It is no answer to say that what the priest does, he does in virtue of Christ having done it. He professes to offer Christ as a Sacrifice to the Father. This rather implies that he does *not* claim that his work is independent of Christ's work. At any rate, this is not, in our Article, laid to his charge. It would be strange, indeed, if his offering of Christ

[1] This seems to have been sometimes virtually denied.

'Epistola ad Hebr. diserte et expresse hoc agit, et sæpius repetit, Christum se ita semel pro peccatis obtulisse, ut non necesse habeat quotidie pro peccatis offerre, nec ut sæpius semetipsum offerat: sicut Leviticus Pontifex, per singulos annos intrabat in sancta. Pighius dicit, *Christum quidem seipsum non offerre sæpius: sed hoc non obstare, quo minus per sacerdotes sæpius offeratur.* (Chemnitz, 'Examen Conc. Trid.,' p. 404. Berlin, 1861.)

Pighius must have been very sensible of the weakness and insufficiency of the usual method of reconciling the Romish Mass with the Epistle to the Hebrews. But his own notion (as reported by Chemnitz) comes clearly under the condemnation of the Council of Trent, which declares, 'Una eademque est hostia, *idem* nunc *offerens* sacerdotum ministerio, qui seipsum tunc in cruce obtulit sola offerendi ratione diversa.' (Sess. XXII., cap. ii.)

should be independent of Christ's offering. But Christ's offering once for all excludes all future sacrificial offering. And if it is the glory of that offering to have been a full, perfect, and sufficient oblation and satisfaction, it is fearfully dishonoured by any attempt or pretence to offer it again or to continue the oblation. If it has completed and finished the work of propitiation, it cannot but be a blasphemous fable to attribute to the priest's work remission of pain or guilt. And the charge of dangerous deceit will not be removed by pleading that the priest's offering of propitiation derives all its virtue from the propitiation of Christ's offering. Christ's sacrificial oblation, if perfect, leaves no room for any other sacrificial oblation, and cannot but be dishonoured by an attempt to introduce it.

Once for all the kingdom of Heaven has been opened to all believers. Its gates have not been shut again to be daily reopened by a priestly immolation.[1] Once for all has the great debt of sin been paid. Who shall presume to pay it again, or add to the payment? Once for all has the great Ransom price been laid down, and

[1] 'Virgo Maria solum semel aperuit Cœlum, sed sacerdos quolibet die, et in qualibet missa.' (Vincentius de Valentia, 'Serm. Æstiv.' Antv., 1572. In 'Fest. Corp. Christi,' Serm. I., p. 322. Quoted by Jewel, Works, P.S. Edit., Harding, 'Thess.,' p. 747.)

Redemption been perfectly won. Who shall dare to lay down the price again, or make more perfect the reconciling work?

It may be, as it has been, urged, that after the perfect work of Christ there remains room for its application; that when the inspired writer says, 'Where remission of these is, there is no more offering for sin,' he does not exclude the application of that remission. This is true, indeed. It needs to be applied—but how? 'By another offering—the oblation of the Mass,' pleads the Romish apologist. But where is a word to be found in the Scripture to suggest or to warrant the notion of applying to man the benefits of One Sacrifice by offering another to God, or by an oblation of the same in another form and after another manner? The inspired words, 'no more offering,' would certainly have been qualified if the Scripture had meant to teach us of any such method of application. As it stands, the unqualified assertion excludes all sacrificial offering for sin, and therefore all offering for application, as much as any offering for any other purpose whatever.

Holy Scripture knows one, and one only, Sacrifice which avails for the remission of sins. Our Church proclaims the Scriptural truth that there is none other satisfaction for sin but that alone. There is no room for any other oblation for sin. The door is shut against every other propitiatory sacrifice. If such a sacrifice asks for admission, there needs no inquiry as to its being dependent or independent. It is needless to ask whether it claims to be applicatory[1] or not applicatory. It is useless to inquire whether it calls itself *absolute* or *relative*. Whether the answer be 'Yea' or 'Nay,' it is equally to be excluded.

In view of this, let the Massing-priest only profess that he offers Christ, and makes a true, proper, and propitiatory sacrifice for the living and the dead; it is enough. However loudly it may be proclaimed that this sacrifice only honours the Sacrifice of the Cross, from which it derives all its efficacy, the plea avails nothing at all. This sacrifice is a derogation from the honour of the one only all-sufficient Sacrifice of Christ. It turns aside men's faith from the one

---

[1] There is, of course, no objection to the term *Applicatory Sacrifice*, understood as including the sense of a feast upon a sacrifice. But it needs to be clearly seen that here the application is by partaking of the benefits of a sacrifice already offered and accepted, not by *offering* of sacrifice at all.

On the confusion of ideas brought in with the teaching of Application of Sacrifice by sacrifice, see 'Romish Mass and English Church,' pp. 31-35. See also Bishop Patrick's Works, vol. viii., pp. 254, 255, Oxford Edit.

only perfect Atonement for sin. If the Word of God is a true word, if the testimony of our Church is a faithful testimony, such a sacrifice cannot escape the condemnation of being a very dangerous deceit.

The sentence cannot be turned aside by parrying a charge which is not down in the Articles of accusation. However earnestly it may be pleaded, however clearly it may be proved that the offering is in a different manner from the offering of the Cross, and that its propitiation is made in a different way from the propitiation of the Death of Christ, all this is *nihil ad rem.* Who ever laid it to the charge of the Mass that it was otherwise—except, perhaps, in popular and too natural misapprehension?

Will anyone deny that the Sacrifices of Masses, according to the teaching of the Church of Rome, contain an offering of Christ for the quick and the dead? Will any say that they are not for the remission of *pœna* or *culpa?* If not, the only charge we make against them remains unanswered. Their defence has broken down. Their position is indefensible. If Christ was once offered to bear the sins of many, and if it be true that by one offering He hath perfected for ever them that are sanctified, then, indeed, must the Sacrifices of Masses be blasphemous fables and dangerous deceits. They must pass away before the light of God's truth, even as the dreams of the night pass away before the brightness of the morning sunshine.

Can any who know anything of the writings of our Reformers, and the principles of the English Reformation, really persuade themselves that our Article was not intended to condemn, and does not actually condemn, that which is held in common by all schools of the Romish communion?

Does not the Article speak the language, and, in its natural and obvious sense, express the views of our English Reformers?

At the date of its composition, what words could have been used to express more clearly than it does the doctrine which it condemns, and the strength of its condemnation?

Can we believe that our Reformers would not have condemned, that in our Article they have not condemned, and condemned with the severest condemnation, even the most minimized form of the Romish doctrine of the Mass?

Nay, further, is it quite certain that they would not have condemned, or, rather, is it not quite certain that they would have condemned, and condemned with even the same condemnation, some few among ourselves (let it be said with all sadness of sorrow) who are teaching a doctrine which they certainly never learnt from such divines as Brevint and Bull, as Jeremy Taylor and Patrick (men who have made their names known as scarcely less strong in defence of the Eucharistic Sacrifice than zealous in denouncing the Romish Sacrifices of Masses); but rather from such as Veron and Bossuet and Du Pin, men who, with all their honest desires to take away stumbling-blocks out of our way, and remove everything which is an offence to our faith, still (as consistent Roman Catholics) insist on the hypostatic oblation of the Body and Blood of Christ, and that for the quick and dead, to have (in some sort) remission of pain or guilt?

Is it a time to take down our fences, and break through the safeguards of our Reformed faith?

It *is* a time for us to seek very earnestly that our souls may be more and more stablished and grounded and rooted in the faith—the faith of a Risen and Ascended Saviour; Risen because of the perfect work which He has accomplished in His death—the faith which leaves no room for the Sacrifice of the Mass.

It is the light of Divine truth which is to scatter the darkness of 'dangerous deceits.' It is in upholding that truth that we are to seek to gain the victory in our controversy with error. Well has it been said: 'We may learn from St. John what is the purest, noblest form of Christian polemics. It is that which contends against its opposite rather by means of the power attending a disclosure of the truth in its beauty than by positive assault, and this accomplishes much more than is effected by the latter method, because positive attacks generally call forth and embitter what is sinful in man, while the mere unveiling of the truth makes common cause with what is good in the hearts of the adversaries themselves, and thus enlists them among its friends and defenders.' (Olshausen, Intro. to Com. on St. John.)

We may not, indeed, withhold our witness against the error of the Sacrifice of the Mass. But for the power of our witness we must trust to our upholding in faith and love the truth of the Sacrifice of the Cross.

Let the Divine miracle of Atonement be a reality to the sinner's faith, and what reality can there be in the Sacrifices of Masses?

Let there be a true reality in faith's view of sin's ten-thousand-talents debt, and reality, too, in the view of that debt quite paid, and of the price which it cost to pay it; let faith's opened eyes look to the Blood of the Lamb; let faith with enlightened eyes behold the Incarnate Son of God on the accursed Cross (being made a curse for us, bearing our sins in His own Body on the tree); let the sinner's faith apprehend the wondrous truth of the One Sacrifice once offered; let the soul stand amazed at the reality of the full, perfect, and sufficient sacrifice, oblation, and satisfaction for the sins of the whole world; let there be reality in the view of the rent veil and the 'open door'; let there be reality in the great transition, in the coming out from condemnation and death to justification and life; let there be reality in breathing the new atmosphere of what we have as those who have passed 'through the gates,' passed from 'under the law' to 'under grace'; reality in the assurance that in Christ we have redemption through His Blood, even the forgiveness of sins; reality in the joyful sense of the liberty wherewith Christ hath made us free, and then all reality must pass away from any idea of propitiatory sacrifice offered by the Mass-priest for the remission of *pœna* or *culpa* for the living or for the dead.

Was it not the view of this blessed reality which taught our Reformers to know that the axe must be laid to the root, not of the teaching of Aquinas, but of the doctrine of Rome?

It is the doctrine of the Mass-Sacrifice itself which is the root of the evil. The abuses of the Middle Ages were the fruit, the evil fruit, which not unnaturally grew upon the branches. We are not to be digging about and dunging the root, while desiring to be also plucking off the fruit. This is what our Church would have done if, as our new teachers would have us believe, she had meant our Article to speak only of the doctrine afterwards connected with the name of Catharinus. But our Church has been taught another lesson in the solemn words of warning which have come down to us from the pen of Archbishop Cranmer: 'The rest is but branches and leaves, the cutting away whereof is but like topping and lopping of a tree, or cutting down of weeds, leaving the body standing, and the roots in the ground; but the very body of the tree, or rather the roots of the weeds, is the Popish doctrine of Transubstantiation, and of the Real Presence of Christ's Flesh and Blood in the Sacrament of the Altar (as they call it), and of the Sacrifice and oblation of Christ, made by the Priest for the salvation of the quick and the dead, which roots, if they be suffered to grow in the Lord's vineyard, they will overspread all the ground again with the old errors and superstitions.' (Pref. to 'Lord's Supper,' 1550.)

If these words are true, they should be set down to no fervour of *odium theologicum*, but to the truest Christian charity. Let it be remembered they are the words of one who died at the stake witnessing for this truth, and deeply repenting of the weakness which had once gainsaid it, and at the same time earnestly exhorting to brotherly love. (See Jenkyns's 'Cranmer,' vol. iv., pp. 137, 139, 140, and Hook's 'Lives,' N. S., vol. ii., p. 416.)

And so as regards our Article, if its declaration is true, its teaching should be set down, not to any unworthy motive pertaining to the heat of a past controversy, but to the zeal of a Christian charity earnestly contending for the faith once delivered to the saints.

And the feeble endeavour made in this tractate to uphold the natural meaning of the Article may fitly be brought to a conclusion in the words of the same wise and learned Archbishop : 'Faxit Deus Omnipotens ut uni Christi sacrificio vere innitamur, ac illi rursus rependamus sacrificia nostra, gratiarum actionis, laudis, confessionis Nominis sui, veræ respiscentiæ ac pœnitentiæ, beneficentiæ in proximos, aliorumque omnium pietatis officiorum. Talibus enim sacrificiis exhibebimus nos nec in Deum ingratos, nec Christi sacrificio indignos.' (Jenkyns's 'Cranmer,' vol. iv., pp. 20, 21.)

APPENDIX.

Note A.—The Multiplicity of the Mass-Sacrifice - page 89.
„ B.—Statements of English Divines - - - „ 94.
„ C.—Remission of Pain or Guilt - - - „ 101.
„ D.—Albertus Magnus - - - - - „ 104.
„ E.—Thomas Aquinas - - - - - „ 107.
„ F.—The Efficacy of the Mass *ex opere operato* „ 115.
„ G.—Catharinus - - - - - - „ 117.
„ H.—Liturgical Changes - - - - - „ 120.
„ I.—The Minimized View of Propitiation - „ 120.
„ J.—The Mass Compared to Prayer - - - „ 125.

NOTE A. (*See* p. 11.)

THE MULTIPLICITY OF THE MASS-SACRIFICE.

THE following quotations will serve to justify our Reformers in speaking of the ' Sacrifices ' in the plural :

'Unum, id est, una forma confectum, et tamen plura sunt Sacrificia.' (Gloss ' On *Unum est corpus*,' in Gratian. Decr., Par. III., ' De Consec. Dist.,' II., Can. LII., p. 1279. Venet., 1567.)

'Favet huic doctrinæ communis fidelium sensus, qui *plura* pro se et suis Sacrificia offerri curant, quod certe non facerent, si infinitam in singulis efficaciam agnoscerent . . . Frustra pro uno defuncto tot *multiplicarentar* Sacrificia, quia unum sufficiens esset ad omnes animas liberandas.' (Bona, ' Tract. Asc. de Missa.,' § 4, Op., p. 107. Antw., 1723.)

'In pluribus missis multiplicatur sacrificii oblatio.' (T. Aquinas, ' Sum.,' Par. III., vol. ii., Quæst. LXXIX., Art. VII., p. 279. Lugd., 1663.)

See also Alanus, 'De Euch. Sacrif.,' lib. ii. (p. 584; Antwerp, 1576), 'plura sacrificia esse videantur.'

A Roman Catholic Divine says: 'The term "Sacrificia Missarum" is equally correct, and has the same meaning with "Sacrificium Missæ." (*Weekly Register*, December 9, 1865. See Blakeney's 'Common Prayer,' p. 122, third edition.)

It is not pretended that all mediæval doctors would have used just the same language. Thomas Waldensis wrote: 'Necessitate fidei nostræ constringimur dicere, quod sacrificium altaris est cum varietate locorum, et temporum, sacrificantium quoque, et visibilium specierum, unum sine multitudine, et idem sine mutatione, et eximio modo unum supra omne Judaicum Sacramentum.' ('De Sacr. Euch.,' cap. xxxii., Op. II., f. 55a. Venet., 1571.)

The following examples may suffice for evidence of *iteration* and *repetition*.

They are quotations representing different periods, and doubtless also varying views of Eucharistic doctrine.

'Augustinus: Iteratur quotidie hæc oblatio, licet Christus semel sit passus.' (Lombard, Lib. IV., Dist. XII., Par. II.)

'Licet surgens a mortuis jam non moritur, et mors ei ultra non dominatur: tamen in semetipso immortaliter atque incorruptibiliter vivens, pro nobis iterum in hoc mysterio sacræ oblationis immolatur.' (Synodus Carisiaca. Anno 838. In Mansi, tom. xiv., c. 749.)

NOTE.—For the sense in which such language as this is to be understood ('non tamen in re, sed in similitudine,' Hen. Gorichen), see Field, 'Of the Church,' Appen., Book III., vol. ii., pp. 93, *sqq.*—E. H. S.

'Iteratur autem quotidie hæc oblatio, licet Christus semel passus in carne.' (Paschasius Radb., 'De Corp. et Sang. Dom.,' cap. ix., Op., c. 1578. Paris, 1618. See also cc. 1560 and 1624.)

'*Iteratur* quotidie hæc oblatio . . . Item *iteratur* hoc Mysterium, et hoc ob commemorationem passionis Christi.' (Gratian, Decr.—as from Paschasius Papa—Par. III. 'De

Consecr. Dist.,' II., Can. LXX., p. 1286. Venet., 1567). *Iteratur* autem quotidie hæc oblatio, licet Christus semel passus est.' (*Ibid.*, Can. LXXI.)
'Eadem Christi hostia *iterum iterumque oblata*.' (Lindanus, 'Panop. Evang.,' lib. iv., p. 297. Colon., 1575.) '*Iteramus* quidem eandem Christi hostiam.' (*Ibid.*) 'Hoc nostrum [sacrificium] Christianum ita *repetitur*, ita *iteratur*, ut in quotidianis mysteriis non offeratur aliud, atque Christus in cruce obtulit.' (*Ibid.*) 'Repetitur igitur una illa Christi hostia, sed non ut Levitica.' (*Ibid.*)
'Hoc [sacrificium] . . . unum, *sæpius* tamen *repetitum*, quia sæpe eo indigemus.' (Contreras, in Theiner, 'Acta Concil. Trid.,' tom. ii., p. 64.)
'Licet pluries offeratur in Missa Christus, non tamen sæpe Christus meretur.' (Ramirez, in *Ibid.*, p. 65.)
See also Theiner, vol. i., p. 610, 'Hoc quotidie iteratur,' and p. 628, 'ideo repetitur oblatio,' and p. 631, 'Sacrificium altaris reiteratur,' and p. 642, 'licet repetantur oblationes.'
'Videmus Apostolum non excludere quamlibet iterationem oblationis Christi, sed eam solam, quæ mortem ipsius requirit.' (Bellarmine, 'De Missâ,' Lib. I., cap. xxv. 'De Controv.,' tom. iii., c. 1030.)
So Cassander had said, 'Constat manifestam esse calumniam, qua insimulatur præsens Ecclesia quod itere oblationem Christi semel factam in cruce, et iterum Christum mactet et crucifigat.' (Consultatio, 'De Iteratione,' Op., p. 1000. Paris, 1616.)
The following is from Alanus, 'De Euch. Sacrif.,' Lib. II., p. 584 (Antwerp, 1576): 'Admirabili modo repetitam passionem,' and p. 577, 'continuo iterabile,' and p. 548, 'eadem mactatione admirabiliter repetita.'
But the following from Bellarmine is specially to be observed: 'Si Patres putassent Sacrificium Eucharistiæ non esse sacrificium, nisi representativum, nunquam dixissent in numero multitudinis, offerri Deo victimas, et sacrificia in altari . . . sed solum in singulari, sacrificium. Unum enim tantum est, quod repræsentatur: et ideo nomen

ejus non potest nisi in singulari efferri.' (' De Controv.,' tom. iii., c. 1009; Ingolst., 1601. 'De Missâ,' lib. i., cap. xv.) It may be well to add that an answer to Bellarmine's argument will be found in Barnes, as quoted by Forbes, in 'Considerationes Modestæ,' vol. ii., p. 594, A. C. L.

The following is from Hugo de Sancto Victore : 'Quæritur : utrum Christus quotidie immoletur. Solutio : Qui semel occisus est in ara crucis : immolatur quotidie in memoriam ipsius passionis in sacramento; nec repetitur ex suâ infirmitate, sed nostra, qui quotidie peccamus, et venalium remissionem consequimur, et augmentum virtutum si digne participamus.' (Annot. Elucid. cir., 1 Cor., Quæst. 98, Op., tom. i., fol. 215b. Venetiis, 1588.)

' Hostiæ legales, ut dicit Apostolus, si perfectos facerent offerri cessarent: unde quæritur, cur hostia salutaris novi testamenti cum perficiat, et sanctificatos consummet, sæpius offeratur, et offerri non cesset. Solutio : semel quidem oblata per passionem mortis in ara crucis in forma humana est: nec iterum sic per mortem offertur: sed tamen in sacramento sæpius offertur: non causa suæ infirmitatis, sed potius nostræ, quia quotidie peccamus : et præcipue propter recordationem mortis Christi, ut amor Ejus cordibus nostris altius infigatur per hoc, quod memores sumus tanti beneficii.' (*Ibid.*, cir. Ep. ad Heb., fol. 237a.)

Dens writes : 'Vi verborum Christus sub speciebus producitur modo quodam mortuo, atque iterum immolatur.' (Dens, 'Tract. Theol.,' p. 366. Dublin, 1812.)

'... Cum ... pro eadem anima sæpius Sacrificium Missæ iteretur.' (*Ibid.*, p. 382.)

' Non omnis culpa in unoquoque Sacrificio remittitur, alioquin perperam pro eodem defuncto pluries offeretur sacrificium.' (*Ibid.*, p. 373.)

Aquinas had thus dealt with this subject : ' Quod sacerdos plures hostias consecrat in una Missa, non multiplicatur effectus hujus sacramenti ; quia non est nisi unum sacrificium. ... In pluribus vero Missis multiplicatur sacrificii oblatio. Et ideo multiplicatur effectus sacrificii et sacramenti.' ('Summa,' Par. III., vol. ii., Quæst. LXXIX., Art. VII.)

On the distinction to be drawn between the *iteration* of the scholastic Divines, and that of the subsequent Romish theology, and especially on the view of Aquinas, see ' Romish Mass and English Church,' pp. 51-54. See also pp. 38-41.

It must not be supposed that the iteration of the Mass-Sacrifice involves of necessity the idea of a repetition of the Sacrifice of the Cross.

Durandus says: 'Licet Christus semel credentes suû morte redemerit, Ecclesia tamen hoc sacramentum quotidie *repetit* . . . Quotidianum sacrificium . . . est commemoratio, non iteratio passionis.' (' Rationale Div. Off.,' Lib. IV., cap. xlii., p. 274. Neap., 1859.)

Bellarmine writes: 'Valor Sacrificii Missæ est finitus. Hæc est communis sententia Theologorum : in quo distinguitur a Sacrificio Crucis—quod infinitæ virtutis erat, et nunquam repetitur.' (Lib. II., ' De Missâ,' cap. iv., § 4.)

NOTE.—In this, Bellarmine differs from Cajetan, Canus, and Scotus. See Morton, ' Of the Inst. of the Sacr.,' p. 482. London, 1635.

It should be added that Cardinal Alan's view of *repetition* is made to stand beside an identity of that which is repeated. 'Hoc sensu dixit Gregorius Hom. 37 in Evang. *Quoties Passionis hostiam offerimus, toties Passionem illius reparamus et pro nobis in Mysterio iterum patitur*, etc. Dicit autem *iterum pati:* et alibi, *iterum immolari:* quia terrena elementa iteratis vicibus commutantur in Corpus immolatum : non quod ipsa immolatio sit alia quam hesterna, aut alia quam fuit in cruce.' (' De Euch. Sacrif.,' Lib. II., p. 553. Antw., 1576. See 'Romish Mass and English Church,' p. 84.)

It may also be added that Bonaventura, after saying 'illud sacramentum iteratur pluries,' explains himself, ' nec dicitur proprie *iterari* sacramentum, sed *frequentari* quoniam unum et idem continetur in hostiâ hesternâ, et hodiernâ.' (In Lib. IV., ' Sent.,' Dist. XII., Par. II., Dub. I., Op., tom. v., p. 145. Lugd., 1668.)

NOTE B. (*See* p. 16.)

STATEMENTS OF ENGLISH DIVINES.

The following extracts will suffice to give evidence of the assertion in the text:

HOOKER.

'Tell not us . . . that ye will read our Scriptures, if we will listen to your traditions; that if ye may have a Mass by permission, we shall have a Communion with good leave and liking. . . . Solomon took it (as well he might) for an evident proof that she did not bear a motherly affection to her child which yielded to have it cut in divers parts. He cannot love the Lord Jesus with his heart, which lendeth one ear to His Apostles, and another to false apostles; which can brook to see a mingle-mangle of religion and superstition, *ministers and massing-priests*, light and darkness, truth and error, traditions and Scriptures. No, we have no lord but Jesus, no doctrine but the Gospel, no teachers but His Apostles.' ('Sermons on St. Jude's Epistle,' Works, vol. iii., p. 666. Edit. Keble.)

WILLET.

'We deny not, but that the sacrament may be called a sacrifice, that is, a spiritual oblation of praise and thanksgiving; but that there is a proper and external sacrifice, as in the law of goats and bullocks, upon the Cross of the Body of Christ; so in the Eucharist, of the same Body and Flesh of Christ, we do hold it for a great *blasphemy* and heresy.' (Willet's 'Synopsis Papismi,' vol. v., p. 352. London, 1852.)

'We hold it to be a great *blasphemy* to say that the priesthood and sacrifice of Christ upon the Cross is not that sacrifice or priesthood into the which the old sacrifice and priesthood was translated and changed.' (*Ibid.*, p. 364.)

'Concerning the name of priests in their sense, as it implieth an authority of sacrificing we utterly *abhor* . . . . To conclude, this word *Priest*, as it is the English of *Sacerdos*, we do not approve; but as it giveth the sense of *Presbyter*,

APPENDIX

from whence it is derived, we condemn it not.' (*Ibid.*, p. 365.)

'They *blasphemously* affirm that it is a sacrifice propitiatory.' (*Ibid.*, p. 368.)

BISHOP BILSON.

'You will have a real, corporal, and local proffering of Christ's flesh to God the Father under the forms of bread and wine made by the priest's external actions and gestures for the sins of such as he list : this is, we say, a *wicked* and *blasphemous* mockery. His passion is the true oblation of the Church ; His flesh wounded and blood shed are the only sacrifices for sin.' ('True Difference,' p. 700. Oxford, 1585.)

BISHOP BABINGTON.

'*It is finished*, and why are we feared? . . . See, see *their sin* that devise a daily sacrifice for sin, either adding unto this most perfect redemption as if it wanted, or else vainly doing by a work of will what already is fully done by prescript of God. . . . The virtue, power, and efficacy of this Sacrifice is perpetual, being once made, and needeth but by faith to be taken hold of and applied.' ('Exposition of Lord's Prayer,' Pet. I., p. 26. London, 1615.)

'The Mass casteth upon our Saviour this reproach, that He is not the only Priest of the New Testament. . . . It overthroweth the merit of His death and passion. . . . The errors and *blasphemies* that are to be found in the Canon of the Mass show how truly detestable it is and ought to be to all faithful men and women ever.' ('Exposition of Cath. Faith,' pp. 255, 256. London, 1615.)

BISHOP FIELD.

'The Fathers most ordinarily, when they make mention of the Supper of the Lord, do term it a sacrifice. . . . Whereupon (by wrested and wrong interpretations) the Papists do build their Sacrifice of the Mass: wherein the priest doth, as they say, offer to God the Sacrifice of Christ's body and blood, *pro vivis et defunctis* . . . and as a *propitia-*

tion for sinners,' etc. ('Parasceve Paschæ,' pp. 206, 207. London, 1624.) 'Saint Augustin saith : " *Tum immolatum fuisse Christum pro nobis, cum in Eum credimus. . . .*" And again : " *Tum pro unoquoque mortuus est Christus, quando pro se mortuum esse illum certo persuasus est. . . .*" So that . . . the Lord's Supper is not *sacrificium,* ἱλαστικὸν, sed ἐυχαριστικὸν.' (*Ibid.*, pp. 211, 212.) 'Not to dwell longer upon these *sacrilegious absurdities* of the Papists.' (*Ibid.*, p. 218.)

MASON.

'Docet Concilium Tridentinum in Missa, *offerri Deo verum et proprium Sacrificium.* . . . Ecclesia Anglicana longe rectius docet. . . . Missas pro vivis et defunctis *blasphemas esse fabulas, et periculosas imposturas.* Hujusmodi igitur sacrificium missaticum, ad Ministros Evangelicos spectare non agnoscimus.' ('Vindiciæ Eccles. Angl.,' Lib. V., cap. i., p. 545. London, 1625.)

'Nos . . . Sacerdotium vestrum missificum, non modo humanum esse commentum, sed etiam in conspectu ipsius Dei viventis *sacrilegum,* et *abominandum* probavimus.' (*Ibid.*, p. 660.)

NOTE.—On Bishop Overall's connection with this work, see ' Papers on Eucharistic Presence,' p. 303.

CRAKANTHORP.

' Quid igitur ? An Christi Corpus, an Ejus substantia in Missâ consumitur ? An Christus (qui vivens est cum offertur) vere et realiter occiditur ? An desinit id esse quod prius erat ? Quam hæc *impia* et *blasphema !*' ('Defensio Eccles. Angl.,' cap. lxxiv., p. 537. A. C. L.)

MEDE.

' The Churches of the Roman Communion " have for many ages disused this oblation of bread and wine, and brought in, in lieu thereof, a real Hypostatical Oblation of Christ Himself. This *blasphemous* oblation we have taken away, and justly."' (Mede, ' The Christian Sacrifice,' chap. viii., Works, p. 376. London, 1677.)

DEAN JACKSON.

'If both the value of the sacrifice be truly infinite, and the virtue of it everlasting, without interruption or discontinuation, more uncessant than the motion of the heavens, or the rest of the earth; the often offering of the sacrifice, after what manner soever, is superfluous and *blasphemous.*' (Works, vol. ix., p. 592. Oxford, 1844.)

J. FORBES, OF CORSE.

'Non enim in eo consistet perpetuitas Sacerdotii Christi, ut semper fiat Ejus vera immolatio, per Sacerdotes, ac si necesse esset Sacerdotium Ejus per mortem extingui, nisi fierent istæ iteratæ sacrificationes in Missi: ut *impie*, et *contra Scripturas*, tradiderunt Tridentini, sess. 22. Sed constat in perpetuo vigore illius unicæ immolationis in passione semel factæ, et perpetua intercessione pro nobis, ad dextram Patris.' ('Inst. Hist. Theol.,' Lib. XI., cap. xx. Op., tom. ii., p. 575. Amsterdam, 1702.)

'Neque opus est alia Oblatione propitiatoriâ, neque ei locus esse potest: nisi (quod cogitatu *blasphemum* est) dicatur Christum illa sui unicâ oblatione non obtinuisse æternam redemptionem credentibus.' (*Ibid.*, p. 571.)

BISHOP HALL.

'That in this Sacred Supper there is a Sacrifice in that sense wherein the Fathers spake, none of us ever doubted. . . . But for any propitiatory sacrifice, unless it be, as the gloss interprets it, representively, I find none. . . . What can either be spoken or conceived more plain than those words of God, *once offered, one sacrifice, one oblation.* . . . While they solemnly offer the Son of God up unto His Father, they humbly beseech Him, in a religious *blasphemy*, that He would be pleased to bless and accept that oblation. . . . We will gladly receive our Saviour, offered by Himself to His Father, and offered to us by His Father: we will not offer Him to His Father. Which one point, while we stick at, as we needs must, we are strait stricken with the thunderbolt of the Anathema of Trent.' (Bishop Hall, 'No Peace with Rome,' Works, vol. ix., pp. 66, 67. London, 1808.)

BISHOP MORTON.

'Lest that there might be any ambiguity, how it doth pacify God, whether by His gracious acceptance, or the efficacy of offering, your General Roman Catechism, authorized both by your Council of Trent, and the then Pope Pius V., from the direction of your whole Church, instructeth you all, concerning your Sacrifice of the Mass, that, *as it is a sacrifice*, it hath *an efficacy and virtue, not only of merit, but also of satisfaction.* So they, as truly setting down the true nature of a *Propitiatory Sacrifice*. . . . Be it known that our Church of England, in her 31st Article, saith of your Propitiatory Sacrifice of the Mass, as it is taught by you, that it is *a blasphemous fable, and dangerous deceit.*' (Bishop Morton, 'Of the Institution of the Sacrament,' Book VI., chap. viii., p. 475. London, 1635.)

BISHOP COSIN.

'Christ can be no more offered, as the doctors and priests of the Roman party fancy Him to be, and vainly think that every time they say Mass they offer up and sacrifice Christ anew, as properly and truly as He offered up Himself in His sacrifice upon the cross. And this is one of the points of doctrine, and the chief one whereof the popish Mass consisteth, abrogated, and reformed here by the Church of England, according to the express word of God.' (Bishop Cosin, 'Notes on P. B.,' 2nd Series, Works, vol. v., p. 333, A. C. L.)

'A true, real, proper, and propitiatory sacrificing of Christ . . . which is the Popish doctrine . . . we hold not, believing it to be a *false* and *blasphemous* doctrine.' (*Ibid.*, p. 336.)

DEAN BREVINT.

'St. Chrysostom is full and eloquent to this purpose . . . *to be offered more than once is an evidence of weakness against the oblation itself*, etc. So Roman Mass is a reproach to the infinite value of Christ's Oblation, being visibly grounded on this plain *blasphemy*, that Christ's oblation on the cross was defective.' (Dean Brevint, ' Roman Mass,' p. 40. Oxford, 1673.)

STILLINGFLEET.

' I do not think any two or three men, though never so learned, make the Church of England ; her sense is to be seen in the public acts and offices belonging to it. And in the Articles . . . your sacrifices on the altar are called *Blasphemous Figments and Dangerous Impostures.*' (Stillingfleet, Works, vol. vi., p. 179. London, 1710.)

BISHOP PATRICK.

' The Church of Rome binds all her members, under pain of eternal damnation, to believe both that the very same body and the very same blood which were once offered by Christ upon the cross, are daily offered up to God by the Mass-priest, and likewise (as if this were not enough) that every such offering made by the priest is a propitiatory sacrifice, nay, makes atonement as well for the dead as for the living.' (Bishop Patrick, Sermon XV., Works, vol. viii., p. 244. Oxford, 1858.)

' This might serve for a short confutation of the Sacrifices of the Mass, as they are commonly called ; but that you may see that our Church was not rash in that sentence it hath pronounced against these sacrifices, as " *blasphemous fables*, and dangerous deceits," I shall a little more distinctly unfold how contradictory they are to the doctrine of the Apostle.' (*Ibid.*, p. 245.)

' There are no such priests in the Church as can offer propitiatory sacrifices to God, for this belongs to Christ alone, who is the sole priest of the New Testament. . . . It is directly against Christ's order, nay, against His office, for any man to go about to offer a proper sacrifice for sin.' (*Ibid.*, p. 246.)

Bishop Bull.

'This proposition ("that in the Mass there is offered to God a true, proper, and propitiatory sacrifice for the living and the dead"), having that other of the "substantial presence of the body and blood of Christ in the Eucharist" immediately annexed to it, the meaning of it must necessarily be this, that in the Eucharist the very body and blood of Christ are again offered up to God as a propitiatory sacrifice for the sins of men. Which is an *impious* proposition, derogatory to the one full satisfaction of Christ made by His death on the cross, and contrary to express Scripture.' (Bishop Bull, 'Corruptions of the Church of Rome,' Sect. III., Works, vol. ii., p. 251. Oxford, 1846.)

Bishop Laney.

'For the sacrifice ... it is, I confess, a word of offence, because there goes under the name of a Christian sacrifice, that which our Church calls a *blasphemous fable* and *dangerous deceit*. ... That which the Article speaks of is the Sacrifice of the Mass, wherein the priests of that sacrifice say, *That Christ Himself is really sacrificed for the quick and dead.*' (Two Sermons preached at Whitehall, pp. 1, 2. London, 1668.)

Bishop Beveridge.

'They all agree in the thing, avouching that in the Mass they offer up a true and perfect sacrifice to God, propitiatory for the sins of the people, even as Christ did when He offered up Himself to God as a propitiation for our sins. This, I say, is that which the Church of Rome confidently affirms, and which our Church in this Article doth as confidently deny.' (Beveridge, 'On Articles,' pp. 506, 507. Oxford, 1846.)

'All the sacrifices of Mass are at the best but *dangerous deceits*.' (*Ibid.*, p. 509.)

Archbishop Sharp.

'The Romanists have invented a new sacrifice, which Christ never instituted, which the Apostles never dreamt

of, which the primitive Christians would have *abhorred*, and which we, if we will be followers of them, ought never to join in.' ('Works,' vol. v., p. 197. Oxford, 1829.)
'This is the Romish doctrine concerning the sacrifice of the Mass. But how groundless, how false, how absurd, nay, how *impious* it is, I now come ... to show.' (*Ibid.*, p. 198.)

JOHN JOHNSON.

'If any have asserted the Sacrifice of the Mass, I would readily grant that no reproaches are too hard, no censures too severe, against them who were guilty of attempting to introduce so *abominable a corruption*.' (Johnson's Works, A. C. L., vol. i., p. 5.)

ARCHBISHOP WAKE.

'If I affirmed the Sacrifice of the Mass to be one of those errors that most offends us, I said no more than what the Church of England has always thought of it.' (Archbishop Wake, 'Defence of Exposition,' p. 67. London, 1686.)

NOTE C. (*See* p. 18.)

'REMISSION OF PAIN OR GUILT [SINNE, 1553].'

The charge had been made against the common opinion of the Mass that it was held to merit remission of *culpa* and *pœna*. Thus, *e.g.*, the *Confessio Variata* of 1540 says: 'Opinio est sparsa in Ecclesiam, quod cœna Domini est opus, quod celebratum a sacerdote mereatur remissionem peccatorum, culpæ et pœnæ, facienti et aliis, idque ex opere operato, sine bono motu utentis' (in 'Sylloge Confess.,' p. 193). See also p. 195: 'Quomodo vivis et mortuis hoc sacrificio promissa sit remissio culpæ et pœnæ,' and again in the 'Apologia Confessionis'—'De Vocabulis Missæ.'

In comparing this with our Article, there are several points of difference, showing the wise caution of our Reformers.

But it is specially to be observed that the Article condemns the teaching of remission by the Mass, not of *pœna* AND *culpa*, but of 'pain *or* guilt.'[1] Some Romish Divines have taught the remission of *culpa* and *pœna* (see Theiner, 'Act. Conc. Trid.,' tom. i., p. 624); some have taught only the remission of *pœna*, especially in the case of the dead (see Theiner, 'Act. Conc. Trid.,' tom. ii., pp. 62 and 119; and Perrone, 'Prœl. Theol.,' tom. iii., p. 236); some only the remission of venial sins (*Ibid.*, p. 64), which brings the sacrifice of a present Christ down to the same level with the sprinkling with holy water (see Melchior Canus, Op., p. 432); while some have recognised its potential efficacy for the remission of all sins, though maintaining that it was not ordained for this purpose (see Theiner, ii., p. 63). Some account of the variety of opinion on this point may be seen in Bishop Morton, 'Of the Institution of the Sacrament,' Book VI., ch. xi., especially sections 1 and 2. See also 'Romish Mass and English Church,' pp. 25 and 30.

The Jesuit Ribera contends for 'an absolute remission of sins,' and appeals to the Council of Trent, 'Ut visibile Sacrificium—quo Cruenti Sacrificii virtus in remissionem peccatorum eorum, quæ quotidie a nobis committuntur applicaretur.' (Com. on Heb. i. 10.)

The following opinions were given by theologians in 1551 before the forming of Canons on the Mass at Trent:

'Est igitur sacra Eucharistia in Missa holocaustum, sacrificium pacificum et propitiatorium, sive pro peccatis, et omnium horum habet usum veritate et virtute, imo in infinitum excedentem: cum ergo Levit. iii., iv., et v. dicitur, quod oblato sacrificio ab eo qui peccaverat, sacerdote rogante pro eo et peccato ejus, dimittebatur ei, quis dubitare potest de hoc sacrificio, in quo solo beneplacitum est Patri, quin eo oblato et orante sacerdote peccata dimittantur? Et officium sacerdotis est offerre dona et sacrificia pro peccatis, et remittuntur per hoc sacrificium non solum

---

[1] It may be noted, however, that the 'Confessio variata' of 1540 does in one place speak as our Article speaks: 'Ergo missa non meretur remissionem culpæ *aut* pœnæ, ex opere operato.' ('Sylloge Conf.,' p. 195.)

peccata venalia et reatus peccatorum remissorum, verum etiam mortalia quoad culpam et pœnam æternam.' (Judicium D. R. Tapperi, Decani Lovaniensis, 'De Sacr. Miss.,' in Le Plat, 'Mon. ad h. Conc. Trid.,' tom. iv., p. 345.) 'Non distinguunt [Protestantes] inter mereri remissionem culpæ et pœnæ, et valere ad remissionem culpæ et pœnæ, sive conferre remissionem culpæ et pœnæ.' (Judicium D. J. a Ravesteyn, 'De Sacr. Miss.,' in Le Plat, 'Mon. ad h. Conc. Trid.,' tom. iv., p. 351). 'Certum est et indubitatum apud Catholicos, sacrificium missæ valere ad remissionem peccati sive culpæ venialis' (*Ibid.*, p. 352). 'Hoc missæ sacrificium non ad venalia tantum abolenda, sed etiam ad mortalia valere omnino existimandum est' (*Ibid.*, p. 353).

Melchior Canus makes mention of three opinions, all of which he rejects : 'Unam, ut oblatio sacra culpas etiam mortales remittere possit. . . Alteram, quæ in remissione peccati nullam vim sacrificio tribuit, nisi ad impetrandam. . . . Tertia sententia est, quæ sacrificium ex opere operato in pœnas valere dicat, in culpas nullo modo' (Op., p. 428 ; Patav., 1734). His own view is thus expressed : 'Vocari in dubium non debet, quin valor missæ ratione quadantenus infinitus sit, hoc est, ad sufficientiam, non ad efficientiam' (p. 432).

But Cardinal Alan argues for the remission of all sins for which Christ died, urging : 'Ego vero nunquam invenio hujus sacrificii usum a Patribus ad pauciora restringi peccata, quam ipsa immolatio Crucis' ('Libri Tres.,' p. 626, Antv., 1576). He quotes from Alexander I. : 'Crimina et peccata his sacrificiis deleri,' and from Julius I. : 'Omne crimen et peccatum sacrificiis Deo oblatis deletur.' And he adds : 'Quam missæ salutarem operationem qui negat, is graves peccatores uno omnium remediorum prestantissimo, et unde eis spes maxima misericordiæ existat, deprivat' (p. 626).

In the Council of Trent it was argued by Aliphanus 'Non minus fuit expiatoria oblatio Cœnæ, quam crucis. . . . Et illud Christi Sacrificium non habuit efficaciam a Cruce ; sed a se ipso, cum Christus de per se efficax sit, sicut et sacramentum in missa ex se efficaciam habet, quia et ibi Christus, sed nisi oblatio Crucis facta fuisset, non potuisset nobis applicari' (Theiner, 'Acta Conc. Trid.,' tom. ii., pp. 93, 94). Another Divine urged: 'Neque missa promissio est remissionis peccatorum, sed ipsum sacrificium remissionem peccatorum conferens.' (*Ibid.*, tom. i., p. 625.)

'Alii loquuntur Sacrificium esse quidem valoris infiniti in se seu *intensive*, non autem quoad effectum seu *extensive*.' (Perrone, 'Præl. Theol.,' tom. iii., p. 236.)

Dens teaches: 'Valor hujus sacrificii est quoad sufficientiam infinitus. Non tamen quoad efficientiam.' ('Tract. Theol.,' p. 382. Dublin, 1812.)

Gregory de Valentia says: 'Ex institutione Dominica simpliciter probatum est, sacrificium hoc esse propitiatorium pro peccatis: valet igitur ad remissionem etiam culpæ, quæ proprie peccatum dicitur.' ('De Mis. Sacri.,' Lib. I., cap. v.; 'De Reb. Contr.,' p. 713. Paris, 1710.)

Bona writes: 'In illis, pro quibus tantum offertur, sive vivis, sive defunctis, tanta erit pœnæ remissio, quantam Christus ex suâ misericordiâ taxavit.' ('De Missâ,' cap. i., § 1, Op., p. 106. Antw., 1723.)

NOTE D. (*See* p. 22.)

ALBERTUS MAGNUS.

It can hardly be supposed that Albertus Magnus ever meant to teach that the Sacrifice of the Mass derived its efficacy from itself, independently of the Sacrifice of the Cross. Witness the following: 'Quomodo hoc sacramentum sit in genere sacrificii? ... Tandem videndum est de hujus sacrificii veritate. Istud autem solum est sacrificii veritas, quia omne id, quod signat, abundanter causat, et continet in seipso per gratiam corporis et sanguinis Domini nostri Jesu Christi.' (Op., tom. xxi., Dict. VI., c. i.

APPENDIX 105

Lugduni, 1602. Quoted from Hebert's 'Lord's Supper,' vol. ii., p. 158.)

The following quotations are from a volume of 'Sermones,' without date (about 1470?):

'Nota quod filios Dei nos ab iniquitatibus nostris redemit in cruce: hanc redemptionem promiserat Spiritus Sanctus per os David in Ps. cxxix: "Quia apud Dominum est misericordia et copiosa est apud eum redemptio. Et ipse redimet Israel ex omnibus iniquitatibus suis." Nota quod per copiosam redemptionem ipse Filius Dei intelligitur. Ipse enim erat Redemptor et Redemptio: sicut dicit Apostolus ad Cor. i. 1. Qui factus est nobis Redemptio. Redemptor igitur fuit quia in propria persona nos redemit. Redemptio fuit quia in semetipso hoc accepit per quod nos redemit, sc. pretiosum sanguinem suum. . . . Igitur Dei Filius redemit in cruce genus humanum ex omnibus iniquitatibus suis quas originaliter traxerat a primis parentibus.' (Serm. II. 'de Tempore,' E.)

'Injunxit Deus Pater Filio suo unigenito ut revocaret per sanguinem suum genus humanum, quod et factum est . . . per dolores suos et cruciatus humanum genus ab inferni doloribus eripuit . . . hinc etiam dicit Joh. in Apoc. I. Qui dilexit nos et lavit nos a peccatis nostris in sanguine suo: a peccatis *glo*. originalibus et actualibus. Et nota quod baptismus ecclesiæ virtutem illam quod peccata hominum lavat accepit a sanguine Christi.' (Serm. VI. 'de Tempore,' B.)

'Nota quod per pascha intelligitur quotidiana recordatio passionis Jesu Christi quotidie enim necesse est ut ore animæ manducemus illum verum agnum paschalem, viz., Jesum Christum assum igne passionis.' (Serm. XXXV. 'de Tempore,' T.)

'Crux dominica quæ bene dicitur pretiosa quasi pretio plena. Pretium enim totius mundi pependit in ea.' (Serm. LIX. 'de Tempore,' M.)

The following quotations are from vol. xii. of the works of Albertus of the Lyons edition of 1651:

'Qui permisit se malignorum manibus semel crucifigi,

permittit se quotidie sceleratorum manibus tractari, et immundorum ac inimicorum dentibus in Sacramento lacerari.' (' De Tertiâ Causa Inst.,' Serm. V., Op., tom. xii., p. 257.)
' Se totum in cruce ad solvendum debitum tuum, dedit.' (*Ibid.*, ' De tribus Causis,' Serm. I., p. 249.)
Expounding Heb. x. : ' Corpus autem, quod præ omnibus sacrificiis est quia sine peccato aptasti, id est, aptum et idoneum dedisti uniendo mihi, quod pro omnium redemptione valeat offerri. Psal. lxviii. : *Persecuti sunt me inimici mei injuste : quæ non rapui, tunc exolvebam,* dum scilicet pro debitis omnium sufficiens sacrificium in cruce offerebam.' (*Ibid.*, p. 250.)
' Secundo quæritur, De quibus memoria Domini sit habenda : Et dicendum . . . De præterito, ut nostri Redemptoris qui per nimiam charitatem a morte mala, morte suâ nos liberavit.' (Serm. II., p. 251.)
' Quia adhuc quotidie labimur, saltem in venialibus : ideo pro nobis Christus quotidie immolatur: ut qui semel moriendo mortem devicit, quotidie recidiva delictorum per hæc sacramenta relaxet.' (' De Sanguine Christi,' Serm. XXVII., p. 291.)
' Necesse fuit ad solvendum tantum debitum, et ad liberandum de inferni carcere genus humanum, Filium Dei hominem fieri, omni creaturâ meliorem : et ipsum pro debito hominis occidi, et Sanguinem Ejus fundi.' (' De Sanguine Christi,' Serm. XXVII., p. 291.)
' Hæc pax cum Deo sive reconciliatio, fit per Sanguinem Christi triplici ratione : scilicet, ratione pretii sufficientis, quod in eo pro nostris debitis solvit ; 2. ratione formositatis, qua nos Deo gratos fecit ; 3. ratione gratissimæ Deo charitatis.' (' De Sanguine Christi,' Serm. XXVIII., p. 293.)
' Finaliter sciendum est, quod sacrosanctum corpus Domini nostri Jesu Christi sumi debet in memoriam Passionis, propitiationis, seu reconciliationis, dilectionis, et unionis,' etc. (' Notula,' p. 300.)

NOTE E. (*See* p. 23.)

THOMAS AQUINAS.

The words often quoted as from Aquinas, on which this gross error was founded, were as follows : ' Secunda causa institutionis est sacrificium altaris contra quandam quotidianam delictorum nostrorum rapinam, ut sicut corpus Domini semel oblatum est in cruce pro debito originali, sic offeratur jugiter pro nostris quotidianis delictis in altari, et habeat in hoc Ecclesia munus ad placandum sibi Deum super omnia legis sacrificia pretiosum et acceptum.' ('De Sacr. Altaris.,' Opusc. lviii. ; Op., tom. xvii., p. 42, col. 2 of second set of paging. Edit. Venice, 1593.)

But it must not be hastily inferred that this language was intended to teach what seems to lie on its surface.

As regards the teaching of Aquinas himself, it is perfectly clear that he held and taught that the sacrifice of the Cross was the one propitiation for all sins, actual as well as original.

The following extracts will suffice as evidence of this:

'Ipse Christus per suam passionem aperuit nobis aditum vitæ æternæ.' ('Summa,' Par. III., vol. ii., Quæst. LXXIX., Art. II.)

'Per passionem suam Christus satisfecit pro peccato humani generis ; et ita homo per justitiam Christi liberatus est.' (*Ibid.*, Par. III., vol. i., Quæst. XLVI., Art. I.)

'Passio Christi non solum sufficiens, sed etiam superabundans satisfactio fuit pro peccatis humani generis.' (*Ibid.*, Quæst. XLVIII., Art. II.)

'Idem ipse unus verusque Mediator per sacrificium pacis reconcilians nos Deo.' (*Ibid.*, Art. III.)

'Pretium redemptionis nostræ est sanguis Christi, vel vita Ejus corporalis, quæ est in sanguine, quam ipse Christus exolvit.' (*Ibid.*, Art. V.)

'Passio Christi est propria causa remissionis peccatorum.' (*Ibid.*, Quæst. XLIX., Art. I.)

'"Christus suâ passione meruit nobis introitum regni cœlestis, et impedimentum removit.' (*Ibid.*, Art. V.)

'Passio Christi prodest omnibus, quantum ad sufficientiam et ad remissionem culpæ, et adoptionem gratiæ et gloriæ.' (*Ibid.*, Par. III., vol. ii., Quæst. LXXIX., Art. VII.)

The following quotations will show that the efficacy of the Mass was, in his view, derived from the propitiation of the Cross:

'Quia enim fructu Dominicæ passionis quotidie indigemus, propter quotidianos defectus, quotidie in Ecclesia regulariter hoc sacramentum offertur.... In hoc sacramento recolitur passio Christi, secundum quod ejus effectus ad fideles derivatur.' ('Summa,' Par. III., vol. ii., Quæst. LXXXIII., Art. II.)

'Per hoc sacramentum participes efficimur fructus Dominicæ passionis.' (*Ibid.*, Quæst. LXXXIII., Art. I.)

'Hoc sacramentum habet virtutem ad remittendum quæcunque peccata, ex passione Christi, quæ est fons et causa remissionis peccatorum.' (*Ibid.*, Quæst. LXXIX., Art. III.)

'Nullius peccati remissio fieri potest, nisi per virtutem passionis Christi.' (*Ibid.*, Quæst. LXIX., Art. I.)

'Passio Christi, in cujus virtute hoc sacramentum operatur, est causa sufficiens gloriæ.' (*Ibid.*, Quæst. LXXIX., Art. II.)

'Sacrificia veteris legis illud verum sacrificium passionis Christi continebant solum in figura.... Opportuit ut aliquid plus haberet sacrificium novæ legis a Christo institutum: ut scilicet contineret ipsum Christum passum ... etiam in rei veritate.' (*Ibid.*, Quæst. LXXV., Art. I.)

If now it be asked how the fact is to be accounted for that language should have been attributed to Aquinas, which seems to imply not only that the sacrifice of the Mass is something *distinct* from the Sacrifice of the Cross (which it is in the doctrine of Rome), but also *independent* of it (which is not the doctrine of Rome), it would appear that an explanation must be sought in two directions:

(1) We should note the language of Aquinas on another point. Thus he wrote, 'Sicut pœnitentia data est in remedium actualis, ita baptismus in remedium originalis.' (In 'Lib. Sent.,' Lib. IV., Dist. IV., Art. IV., quoted from Rogers 'On Articles,' p. 278.) It is to be observed how here he attributes to baptism what in the passage before us he attributes to the sacrifice of Christ's death.

And it will hardly be doubted that Aquinas would have reconciled these two sayings by declaring that what was rightly attributed to the Sacrifice of the Cross as the *fountain*, was not wrongly attributed also to the sacrament ordained for the *application* of its benefits. The infant coming in its original sin to baptism had in that sacrament all purged away, *ex opere operato*, by reason of the efficacy of Christ's one oblation once offered.

(2) But it should be marked that a somewhat similar doctrine of *application* had been growing up in the Romish Church in connection with the Eucharist; and that not only in connection with the Eucharist as a sacrament, but also as a sacrifice. It was a strange notion, indeed, that one sacrifice should be applied by the offering of another sacrifice; that after God had provided and accepted one perfect sacrifice for sins, the benefits of that sacrifice should be applied to the souls of sinners by the offering to God of another act of oblation. Perhaps the true account of the development of this idea may be found in the following brief summary. A Christian in early days of primitive Christianity, in the sense of daily need for daily errings, would say: 'Because I am continually sinning, therefore also I ought constantly to receive,' *i.e.*, to receive the merits of Christ's atoning death in the sacrament which He has ordained to be the communion of His body given for me, and His blood shed for the remission of my sins. ('Quia semper pecco, debeo semper accipere medicinam.' See Gratian, 'Dec.,' Par. III., 'De Cons.,' Dist. II., Can. XIII.) Somewhat later on, as the sacrificial aspect of the Eucharist came perhaps into greater prominence, the same idea might

find expression in language more like this, 'Because we are always sinning, therefore we ought to be always offering.' ('Quia quotidie labimur quotidie Christus mystice pro nobis immolatur.' *Ibid.*, Can. LXX. ; see also Can. LXXI.) And this 'offering' doubtless meant at first nothing more than offering to view, or pleading in the Eucharist of remembrance the merits of Christ's death as the one propitiation for sins, perfect in the past. (See below, p. 114.) But as time went on, and superstitions grew apace, efficacy became attributed to the ordained memorial. And the representative signs in their signification were looked to as availing for the same purposes as the things signified by them. And the memorializing act of the priest came to be regarded as in itself a sacrifice, and the proximate object of faith, the Sacrifice of the Cross being behind it. ('Providens Dominus nobis dedit hoc sacramentum salutis, ut quia nos quotidie peccamus, et ille jam mori non potest, per istud sacramentum peccatorum remissionem consequamur.' *Ibid.*, Can. LXXII.)

It is well known how Gregory the Great spoke : ' In ipsa immolationis horâ ad sacerdotis vocem, cœlo aperiri . . . angelorum choros adesse, summis ima sociari, terrena cœlestibus jungi, unumque ex visilibus et invisilibus fieri.' ('Dialog.,' Lib. IV., cap. lviii., Op., tom. ii., c. 472. Venet., 1744.)

And again : 'Adhuc per hanc in suo mysterio iterum patitur. Nam, quoties Ei hostiam suæ passionis offerimus, toties nobis ad absolutionem nostram passionem illius reparamus.' ('In Ev.,' Lib. II., Hom. XXXVII., § 7, tom. i., c. 1631. *Cf.* Gratian, 'De Cons.,' Dist. II., Can. LXXIII.)

And if somewhat of this may be set down to hyperbolical expressions overleaping the limits of the teaching intended to be conveyed, it cannot be doubted that Gregory entertained the notion of an 'objective magical operation of the sacrifice for the quick and dead.' (See Neander's 'Ch. Hist.,' vol. v., p. 174. Clark.) And this notion afterwards received additional strength when the doctrine of the corporal presence on the altar took hold of men's minds. Algerus did not hesitate to say : ' Hinc ergo pensemus quale sit pro nobis sacrificium, quod pro absolutione nostra passionem unigeniti Filii imitatur. Quamvis ergo non dixerit [Gregorius] passionem unigeniti operatur vere, sed imitatur imaginarie, tamen testatur illam victimam, nos vere ab æterno interitu salvare.' (' De Sacr. Euch.,' Lib. I., fol. 46a. Friburgi, 1530.)

And Aquinas affirms : ' Quoties hujus hostiæ commemoratio celebratur, opus nostræ redemptionis exercetur.' ('Summa,' Par. III., vol. ii., Quæst. LXXXIII., Art. I., p. 333. Ludg., 1663.)

After this it was no marvel that the priest was regarded as offering a propitiatory sacrifice, able to take away culpa or pœna, *ex opere operato*, although the *work wrought* would doubtless be understood as deriving its efficacy from the Cross, and would be explained as like drawing water in a vessel from a deep well of Divine Grace—from the fountain once opened for sin by the sacrifice of Christ. (See Lindanus, ' Panop. Evang.,' Lib. IV., p. 297. Colon., 1575; and especially Perrone, ' Prælec. Theol.,' vol. iii., p. 240. Paris, 1856.)

It was but a step beyond this when men came to regard it as one of the causes of the institution of the Eucharist that the Church might have an oblation wherewith to propitiate God for daily infirmities.

And this language, misleading as it was, would certainly have been explained by Aquinas, as speaking only of that which was proximate (in his view) to the faith of the Christian man, as telling only of the efficacy of application —the application of that which was derived only from the atoning sacrifice of Christ.

The following is Bellarmine's explanation of the language of Aquinas :

' Sed video unde Philippus occasionem arripuerit mentiendi, et calumniandi, quia videlicet S. Thomas in opusculo, De Sacramento Altaris, cap. i., docet ; Corpus Domini semel oblatum in cruce pro debito originali, jugiter offerri in altari pro debitis quotidianis. At Sanctus Thomas non dicit, in cruce pro solo debito originali oblatum Christi Corpus, imo etiam pro actualibas oblatum docet. 3 par., 9, 1, Art. IV. ; et 9, 49, Art. I., ad 4. Id ergo in eo opusculo sibi voluit S. Thomas, quia peccatum originale semel dimissum nunquam repetitur, ideo ad illum expiandum non esse necessaria quotidiana sacrificia, sed sufficere sacrificium crucis semel peractum, et semel per Baptismum applicatum. At pro peccatis actualibus, quæ sæpius committuntur, instituta esse, præter Baptismum quotidiana remedia, in quibus sacrificium altaris merito numeretur.' (' Judicium de Libro Concordiæ ;' XVIII. Mendacium, Op., tom. vii., c. 605. Colon., 1617.)

This is, indeed, a somewhat lame apology for the very misleading language which it defends — language which Melancthon was surely justified in regarding as (to say the least) leading not unnaturally to gross popular errors.

But let the words of Catharinus, as quoted by Bishop Jewel (see below, Note G., p. 116), be set beside the language of Aquinas, and it will be seen at once how they tend to confirm the view we have taken of his meaning. Indeed, the language of both will mutually give and receive explanation by comparison.

The older teaching of a commemorative sacrifice—the commemoration of the One sacrifice, a pleading of the merits of the One finished propitiation—still stood beside the newer teaching of a proper and propitiatory sacrifice offered by the priest on the altar. But the newer teaching was being made to overshadow the older, and (in the popular mind, at least) was doubtless tending to hide it. Still, the older doctrine could not be displaced, and the teaching of the older and the newer were brought into forced reconciliation by this doctrine of application. (See Litton, ' Dogmatic Theology,' p. 298.)

And certainly such language as that attributed to Aquinas and Catharinus, though its gross error may be eviscerated by explanation, was bearing witness to the dangerous fruit which would naturally grow on this complicated and misleading doctrinal system. It bears witness to the great need there was for the work of the Reformation, and to the need that the doctrine of the Reformation should insist on the truth that when Christ overcame the sharpness of death He opened the kingdom of heaven to all believers, and that the doors had not since been shut to be re-opened day by day by the Mass-priest in his oblation; that all that was needed to be done for man's reconciliation had been accomplished by the Cross, and that the only application required was the application of the believer's faith accepting the reconciliation of God.

In all this doctrine of application of the Sacrifice of the Cross by the offering of the sacrifice of the Mass what is prominent is the work of the priest (as a representative of Christ), and what is out of view is the faith of the sinner in the doctrine of the Cross.[1] And, though there may be in the teaching of theologians a repudiation of the popular and natural abuse which looks for the effect 'sine bono motu utentis,' yet in the *bonus motus* required we look in vain for the conversion of the soul to God by the faith of the crucified Saviour.

'Fides nostra,' says Bishop Jewel, 'mortem et crucem Christi nobis applicat, non actio sacrificuli. "Fides," inquit Augustinus, "sacramentorum justificat, non sacramentum." Et Origines: "Ille," inquit, "est sacerdos, et propitiatio, et hostia, quæ propitiatio ad unumquemque venit per viam fidei." Atque ad hunc modum, sine fide, ne vivis quidem prodesse dicimus sacramenta Christi; mortuis vero multo minus.' ('Apol. Eccl. Angl.,' p. 14. P.S. edit.)

It would appear that the corruption of the truth had struck its roots into the mistaken notion that if in the Eucharist there was to be a partaking of—a feeding upon—

---

[1] 'Nec refert, quod tantum ad aliquos effectus requiratur dispositio ex parte suscipientis; non enim requiritur ut ratio formalis causandi, sed solummodo ut conditio, sicut in sacramentis.' (Dens, 'Tract. Theol.,' p. 371. Dublin, 1812. See 'Syll. Confes.,' pp. 193, 283. and especially Chemnitz, 'Examen,' Par. II., sec. vi., pp. 250-253. Berlin, 1861.)

a sacrifice, then the sacrificing act itself must be found in the Eucharistic service. A correction, indeed, of this error may be found in the writings of some more enlightened divines of the Romish Communion, as, for example, in the teaching of Ferus (whose works were put on the Index): 'In ecclesia autem sacrificium nostrum est Christus, qui semel quidem Seipsum obtulit, memoria tamen et representatio Ejus sacrificii quotidie in Ecclesia fit. Juxta hoc offerre debemus sacrificium laudis, item sacrificium justitiæ, imo nosipsos.' ('In Gen.,' cap. viii., p. 248. Colon., 1572. See Waterland's Works, vol. v., p. 235.)

Contarini's teaching on the point was not dissimilar (see 'Christi. Instr.,' Interro. 17, Op., p. 536. Paris, 1571), his 'oblatio, qua offerimus Christum, Ejusque passionem,' being understood (see Waterland, vol. v., pp. 269, 275) in the ancient sense of 'offering to view' representatively, and pleading before God. But his teaching ('De Sacramentis,' Lib. II., Op., pp. 358 *sqq.*) should also be taken into view.

And even Cajetan seems to have taught very much the same doctrine. (See Canon Jenkins's valuable work, 'Pre-Tridentine Doctrine,' p. 99. See also p. 83, where Canon Jenkins's criticism should be noted, and p. 84.)

Waterland quotes from the 'moderate Roman Catholic,' Barnes: 'Capiendo sacrificium passive, pro sacrificato, noviter applicato nobis, asseritur rite sacrificium missæ.' (Works, vol. v., p. 236.)

See also quotations in Forbes, 'Considerationes Modestæ,' vol. ii., pp. 590-596. These divines, of course, denied *iteration* of the sacrifice (see pp. 590, 594), as did also Nic. de Lyra, who wrote 'Non est ibi sacrificii iteratio, sed unius sacrificii in cruce oblati quotidiana commemoratio.' ('In Heb. x.,' c. 904, 'Bibl. Sac. cum Gloss. Ord.' Ludg., 1589.)

On the sacrificial doctrine of divines before Luther's time, see Field, 'Of the Church,' vol. ii., pp. 72-95.

APPENDIX

NOTE F. (*See* p. 36.)

THE EFFICACY OF THE MASS 'EX OPERE OPERATO.'

I am indebted to Bishop Wordsworth for the reference to Pighius. See his able and learned 'Responsio ad Batavos,' p. 7.

When the Bishop adds, concerning Pighius, 'Sed nihilominus doctrinam missas ex opere operato valere subtiliter defendit,' he must not be understood to imply that in this Pighius was transgressing the limits of accredited Roman theology. It is true that this phrase is not applied by the Trent Council to the efficacy of the Mass-sacrifice. It is true also that some divines of reforming tendencies are anxious to clear the doctrine of the Mass from a doctrine of *opus operatum*, which might seem to make it independent of the sacrifice of the Cross. Witness the following from Gaspar Contarini, repudiating the charge of Lutherans: 'Quasi opus illud operatum sacerdotis æquiparetur Christi passioni, et quod nobis remittantur peccata non tantum per Christi oblationem, et *unum* illud *verum sacrificium*, sed etiam per *opus operatum* sacerdotis.' ('De Sacram.,' Lib. II., Op., p. 358. Paris, 1571. See also Cajetan as quoted in Jewel, 'Apol. and Defence,' p. 557, P.S. edit.; and Field, 'Of the Church,' vol. ii., p. 74, E. H. S.)

But it must by no means be supposed that the Romish doctrine of the Mass, as taught by her theologians, knows no sacrificial efficacy *ex opere operato*. Witness the following: 'Firmiter tenendum est, missam divinum esse institutum . . . *verum est sacrificium*, vivis plurimum conducens et defunctis in peccatorum remissionem et satisfactionem. Excellenti enim innititur merito passionis Christi, unde virtus procedit sacramentorum. Quare non solum ex devotione valet celebrantis, sed præcipue ex virtute et merito Christi, quod ibi applicatur ex Ejus ordinatione, et a plerisque *opus operatum* solet appellari.' (Facult. Theol. Parisiensis, 'Ep. ad Regem.,' Ann. 1535; in Le Plat, 'Mon. ad Hist. C. Trid.,' tom. ii., p. 795. Lovanii, 1782.)

'Duplex spectari potest in hoc sacrificio vis effectiva, una quam dicunt Theologi *ex opere operato*, independenter a merito et dignitate Ministri. . . . Primum effectum *ex opere operato* plures Theologi docent, nec sacerdotem percipere ut offerens est, nec fideles quatenus sunt offerentes, sed quatenus pro ipsis offertur. . . . Constans semper fuit Catholicorum sententia, habere hoc [sacrificium] infallibiles et determinatos effectus *ex opere operato*, nisi ille pro quo offertur obicem ponat, remissionem videlicet alicujus pœnæ peccatis jam remissis debitæ, vel donum alicujus gratiæ prevenientis ad obtinendam commissorum remissionem.' (Bona, 'Tract. Asc. de Missa.,' § 3, Op., p. 106. Antv., 1723.)

'Quod colligit, Missam *ex opere operato* non mereri remissionem pœnæ, aut culpæ, magis est frivolum . . . quam ut responsionem mereatur.' (Lindanus, 'Panop. Evang.,' lib. iv., p. 299. Colon, 1575.)

'Cum offertur, prodest ex opere operantis, et *ex opere operato*.' (Gabriel de Ancona in Theiner, 'Acta Concil. Trid.,' tom. i., p. 631.)

'Quamvis de fide non sit, per sacrificium Missæ certo semper seu certa lege pœnam temporalem *ex opere operato* remitti, est tamen certa Theologorum doctrina *ex opere operato* pœnam ejusmodi per sacrificium remitti.' (Perrone, 'Prælec. Theol.,' vol. iii., p. 235. Paris, 1856.)

'Oblatio hujus Sacrificii est fructuosa ex opere operato.' (Suarez, No. 3, Thom., Quæst. LXXXIII., Art. J., Disp. 79, § 8. See Morton on Euch., p. 485.)

'Quod ergo efficit ratione ipsius Corporis Christi et actionis mysticæ circa ipsum, hoc dicitur operari *ex opere operato*.' (Alanus, 'Libri Tres.,' p. 633. Antv., 1576.)

'Sacrificium Missæ causat effectus suos ex opere operato.' (Dens, 'Tract. Theol.,' p. 371. Dublin, 1812.)

It should be well observed that the Council of Trent has given no definition of its sense of *Opus Operatum*, about which there was much diversity of opinion. (See Jewel, 'Harding, Thess.,' P.S. edit., p. 750.) There is a sense in which it was accepted by the Reformed as expressing a

doctrine of the Sacraments not to be questioned. (See
'Doctrine of Sacraments,' pp. 75, 76.) Accordingly, the
condemnation of the term inserted in our Article of 1553
was wisely omitted in 1662.

But this sense stands clearly distinguished from the sense
in which it is commonly used by Romish divines. As applied
by them to the *Sacrifice*, it points habitually to the certain
and invariable efficacy which it is supposed to have by the
sacerdotal service of the priest, from the fact of its being what
it is, or from the institution of Christ, as distinguished from
the uncertain and varying effects resulting (*ex opere operantis*)
from the devotion of the priest.

The *opus operantis* was held to be also propitiatory ' in a
far lower degree of propitiation' (as 'prayer, a contrite
heart,' etc.). See Harding in Jewel's works, 'Harding,
Thess.,' P.S. edit., p. 754.

On the subject generally, see Chemnitz, 'Examen Conc.
Trid. De Sacr.,' § 6, Can. VII., p. 250. Berlin, 1861.

NOTE G. (*See* p. 40.)

CATHARINUS.

The teaching of Catharinus is thus represented by Jewel:
'Apparet quod pro peccatis, sub novo testamento post
acceptam salutaris hostiæ in baptismo efficaciam commissis,
non habemus pro peccato hostiam illam, quam Christus
obtulit pro peccato mundi et pro delictis baptismum præce-
dentibus: non enim nisi semel ille mortuus est; et ideo
semel duntaxat hostia illa ad hunc effectum applicatur.'
('De Incruent. Sacrif. Nov. et Ætern. Test.' in Jewel,
'Apol. Def.,' p. 558, P.S. edit.)

A cognate error appears to have been taught by Cardinal
Osius: 'Christum peccata nostra pertulisse quidem in corpore suo, sed quo ad culpam tantum, quare reliquum esse,
ut nos patiamur quoque in nostro corpore, aut in nostro
marsupio, satisfaciamusque quoad pœnam.' (See Vergerius,
Op., tom. i., fol. 163. Tubingæ, 1563.)

An interesting account of Catharinus and his opinions will be found in Du Pin, 'Eccles. Hist. Sixteenth Cent.,' Book V., pp. 3, *sqq*. (English transl., London, 1706.) Du Pin says he made himself to be taken notice of at Trent 'as well by his capacity as by the opinions which he maintained, which are very different from the common notions of divines' (p. 3). Again: 'He is very free, sometimes even rash, in his assertions, and makes no scruple of leaving the common opinion of divines to walk in new roads. . . . His system of predestination is very extraordinary, and he is followed in it by nobody' (p. 18).

But Du Pin makes no mention of his peculiar doctrine of the Mass, and it is impossible to believe that his unguarded language would not have received from him an explanation (like that of Aquinas) which would have virtually explained away the monstrous notion which it seems too plainly to convey.

Catharinus' treatise is indeed a singular production, and affords striking evidence of the inevitable tendency of the doctrine of applicatory sacrifice to fill the field of vision and fasten the eye of faith on the efficacy of the sacerdotal oblation on earth. Nevertheless, it is quite clear (1) that he did not regard the Sacrifice of the Cross as available *quoad pretium* only for original sin, and (2) that he did regard the Sacrifice of the Mass as deriving its efficacy from the Redemption, purchased by the Atoning Blood of Christ, as once for all offered to bear the sins of many. In his view (saving, of course, the doctrine of sacramental penance) the Sacrifices of Masses are the great object which faith has to look to for remission of post-baptismal sin. But these Masses are certainly not independent of the Sacrifice of the Cross.

The following brief extracts will suffice to give evidence of this:

'Quemadmodum ille inobediens inhonoravit Deum Patrem nescio quid divinum appetens: ita hic noster, abjiciens gloriam Divinitatis suæ, complevit omnem obedientiam in sacrificio carnis suæ, in quâ carne posuit illud peccatum atque omnia scelera et delicta nostra ex eo manantia . . .' (c. 159).

'Solus Christus et unica illa sua cruenta oblatione satisfecit pro peccatis nostris ante primam justificationem' (c. 160, margin).

'Hoc sacrificium est quædam gratiorum actio de jam accepto illo cruento sacrificio ad redemptionem nostram ut statueremur in novo testamento . . . est enim sacrificium novi testamenti, quod præsupponit (ut dixi) redemptionem et acceptationem illius cruentæ hostiæ' (c. 165).

'Sic ergo Christus sua illa sanctissimi corporis cruenta oblatione non abstulit aliis, imo vero attulit (quemadmodum dixi) facultatem similiter sese offerendi' (c. 168).

'Nec nos sine sanguine oblationem offerimus. Et licet hic sanguis quem sensibiliter offerimus nunc, sensibiliter non effundatur hoc tempore: est tamen ille idem sanguis effusus, et secundum vigorem toties effunditur, quoties offertur cum commemoratione effusionis antiquæ' (c. 169).

'Hoc enim sacrificium novum et incruentum suam habet efficaciam ab illo cruento cujus commemoratio fit' (c. 170).

'Primum quod quanquam prima illa cruenta Christi oblatio liberaverit totum mundum ab antiquo peccato et reatu illius, et consequenter ab omni reatu supradictorum peccatorum: attamen (sicut diximus) non ita liberavit, ut non sit necessarium cuilibet applicari merita illius hostiæ (c. 171).

'Illa hostia applicari eis secundum primum modum non potest' (c. 173).

'Ita post oblationem Christi etiam oblationes nostræ non superfluunt, nec adjiciunt ad injuram suæ oblationis, per quam potius sanctificantur' (c. 174).

NOTE.—I am indebted to Bishop J. Wordsworth for the information ('Responsio ad Batavos,' p. 23) that a copy of the treatise of Catharinus was to be found in the Lambeth Library.

NOTE H. (See 'p. 54.)

LITURGICAL CHANGES.

A comparison of the First Book of Edward VI. with the Sarum Missal will show clearly a design of laying low the Sacrifice of the Mass. (See Hutton's 'Anglican Ministry,' p. 192.) But the Revision of 1552 evidenced a more decided determination to clear away ambiguities, and to leave no room for any sacrificial offering of Christ.

In the ordinal, published separately in 1549, the bishop was still directed to ' deliver to each one of them [the priests] the Bible in the one hand, and the chalice or cup with the bread in the other hand.' This was omitted in 1552. But in 1549 had already been removed the mediæval injunction, 'Accipe potestatem offerre sacrificium Deo, missamque celebrare tam pro vivis quam pro defunctis.'

This argument derives additional force from the fact that the Forty-two Articles of 1553 contained a clause (No. XXIX.) which declared ' Non debet quisquam fidelium carnis Ejus et Sanguinis Realem et Corporalem (ut loquuntur) præsentiam in Eucharistiâ vel credere vel profiteri.'

The clause was afterwards wisely omitted, its purpose being sufficiently (and with less ambiguity) secured by the insertion of Art. XXIX.

NOTE I. (See p. 72.)

THE MINIMIZED VIEW OF PROPITIATION.

Veron, insisting that more than this is not *de fide* in the Roman Church, urges that so much can offer no difficulty to our faith, and cannot derogate from the doctrine of the Cross—' Quid facilias creditu tali propitiatione? Et quæ ibi derogatio propitiationi sacrificii crucis?' (' Reg. Fidei,' § 14.)

It is, of course, readily granted that *propitiation* thus reduced to *nil* derogates nothing from the atonement of

Christ. But this minimized propitiation, in Veron's view, is the effect of the sacrifice (though it be not *de fide* that its effect is *ex opere operato*), and the sacrifice requires that Christ should be offered (*in sacrificium offerri*) by the act of the priest, *vere et reipsa*. He asks, ' Quo pacto vere et reipsa in sacrificium offerri dici potest id, circa quod actio sacerdotis offerentis non reipsa, sed tantum similitudine quadam, et in figurâ versatur?' And he quotes from Vasquez words indicating of Christ, ' Quamvis non dicatur reipsa et vere, sed in solâ figurâ et similitudine occidi et mori, tamen vere et reipsa immolari, et in sacrificium offerri dicitur.' And this, we maintain, *is* a derogation from the all-sufficiency of the ' *one* ' and the ' once ' of Christ's sacrifice.

But, further, Veron's language concerning the minimized view of propitiation itself seems to concede that to teach *more than that* might be charged with derogating from the sacrifice of the Cross. And we ask, Has the teaching of *more than that* (as regards propitiation) ever been condemned by the Church of Rome? If not, it is a poor apology for the Church of Rome that she leaves it free on such a point for her doctors to say ' Yea ' or ' Nay.'

It should also be observed that to say of a doctrine that it is not *de fide* is no evidence that its denial may claim approval. ' Ast, licet aliqua doctrina non sit de fide, potest tamen esse fidei proxima certa, etc., quibus respondent *qualificationes*, ut vocant, diversæ ob negatam illam doctrinam, quod ex. gr. propositio sit "proxima hæresi, hæresim sapiens, erronea," etc.' (Perrone, ' Præl. Theol.,' vol. iii., p. 236.)

What we want is the assurance not that more than this is not *de fide*, but that the truth which involves the negation of more than this is *de fide*. Would the negation of more than this be allowed in the Roman Communion? Would the writings of a Divine who should express himself in the language of our Article be approved in the Romish Church? Would a layman maintaining the doctrine of our Article be knowingly admitted to Communion in that Church?

Some, indeed, do seem to think that practically the

present teaching of the Church of Rome rejects all but the most minimized view of the sacrifice. It may be well, therefore, to direct attention to a few brief extracts from a work which has the *nihil obstat* of the censor, and the *imprimatur* of Cardinal Vaughan. 'The sacrifice of the altar was to represent and commemorate that of the cross, and also to supply all that was wanting in the latter.' 'There is a mystical destruction of the Victim, for Christ presents Himself on the altar "as in a state of death" ... Moreover, it fulfils the form and ends of sacrifice. Like the holocausts, it offers homage to God; like the sin-offerings, it propitiates Him by the very fact that it is an oblation of Christ, the Victim for our sins. ... It is truly "propitiatory," and may be offered for the living and dead. ... Consumption of the species forms an integral part of the sacrifice.' ('Catholic Dictionary.' London: Kegan Paul, 1893.)

Yet even this contains little more than the most natural sense of the teaching of the Council of Trent.

And the Tridentine Catechism is even more distinct. 'Ut autem sacrificium est, non merendi solum, sed satisfaciendi quoque efficientiam continet. Nam ut Christus Dominus in passione suâ pro nobis meruit, ac satisfecit: sic qui hoc sacrificium offerunt, quo nobiscum communicant, Dominiœ passionis fructus merentur, ac satisfaciunt.' (Part II., cap. iv., § 78.)

Bona teaches: 'Æque placet Deo, ac mors Ejus in cruce, licet effectus finitus sit.' ('De Missâ,' cap. iii., § 2. Op., p. 110. Antw., 1723.)

Moehler speaks of the 'undoubting faith that Christ before our eyes offers Himself up for us to His eternal Father.' And he says: 'It is one and the same undivided Victim, one and the same High Priest, who on the Mount of Calvary and on our altars hath offered Himself up as an atonement for the sins of the world.' ('Symbolism,' p. 238. Robertson's translation, 3rd edit.)

But let the following also be added from a publication

which has the *nihil obstat* of the censor, and the *imprimatur* of Cardinal Manning.

The language quoted, as being from a book devotional rather than dogmatic, may fairly ask that criticism should scan it through dimmed glasses. But even so, the idea conveyed, recurring again and again, assumes a prominence which can hardly be regarded otherwise than a very dangerous deceit: ' With the penalty of Thy life Thou didst make Thyself a sacrifice on Calvary, and, that it might never be forgotten, every day on Thy altar Thou art again mystically crucified. Every day Thy blood mystically pours afresh from Thy heart, and Thy wounded hands and feet.' ('The Love of Jesus,' by the Rt. Rev. Mgr. Canon Gilbert, D.D., V.G., pp. 40, 41; 37th edit.)

' Was not one atonement . . . one sacrifice, one Calvary, sufficient ? . . . In the midst of Thy passion Thou, O Jesus, foresawest our weakness and our guilt. . . . Thou didst feel that we should contemn Thy first sacrifice, and so . . . every day Thou art sacrificed again.' (*Ibid.*, pp. 47, 48.)

' Make us acknowledge that on this altar Jesus is truly immolated, and that in this church the very same sacrifice is consummated which was offered for the atonement of the world on Calvary.' (*Ibid.*, p. 49.)

' Thy life is offered in oblation and sacrifice for us. And this *not once*, or in one place, but in as many places as there are altars throughout the world. And with Thee, our Saviour, daily crucified and sacrificed on the altar for sin, how can we ever despond or fear?' (*Ibid.*, p. 53.)

' Make us assist at daily Mass, that so the precious blood of the sacrifice may wash away those sins which will so alarm us at the last day.' (*Ibid.*, p. 143.)

' We hold that here in a mystical manner Thy body and blood are separated, and that Thou art, as it were, again nailed to the Cross, and presented to heaven as a holocaust, for the propitiation of the sins of the world.' (*Ibid.*, p. 46.)

And such teaching is not new. Alanus said : ' Inscrutabili modo, vere quoque ac realiter geri, ita ut non sit falsum dicere, Christum mori, occidi, immolari, animam deponere, frangi, et pati multa ... in sacramento, quæ noluit pati in cruce.' ('Libri Tres.,' p. 543. Antv., 1576.) 'Neque hæc summa veritas de Christi immolatione ac mactatione in Eucharistia est ab Ecclesia inventa, aut a nobis conficta.' (*Ibid.*, p. 554. See 'Romish Mass and English Church,' pp. 38-40.)

And De Lugo wrote: 'Corpus Christi . . . destruitur humano modo, quatenus accipit *statum decliviorem* et talem quo reddatur inutile ad usus humanos corporis humani, et aptum ad alios diversos usus per modum cibi. . . . Talis "exinanitio" . . . non solum satis intelligitur ut vere et proprie sacrificalis, sed etiam excepto sacrificio cruento in cruce nullam sublimiorem ac profundiorem rationem veri et proprii sacrificii concipere possumus.' ('De veritate Sacr. Euch.,' Disp. XIX. 5. Lugd., 1636, quoted from Gore's 'Euch. Sacri.,' p. 11.) The following is from a treatise, for which is claimed a high theological reputation at the present day—the 'Professio Fidei Catholicæ' of the *Fratres a Walenburch* (seventeenth century). 'Ut sensus sit calicem effundi pro nobis, qui utique non in cruce, sed in ultima Cœnâ effusus est; sanguine nimirum, qui erat in calice, pro nobis effuso. Cum ergo Christus *pro nobis*, dederit corpus suum, nec alteri dederit, nisi Deo Patri suo, habemus in actione Christi verum et proprium sacrificium; habemus et propitiatorium sacrificium quia Christus seipsum non obtulit pro nobis, nisi ad propitiationem; quod et explicavit dicens—*In remissionem peccatorum.* Et quia dixit sanguinem suum *pro multis* effundi, Ecclesia Catholica intellexit, quod et traditum ab Apostolis accepit, sacrificii incruenti effectum etiam ad defunctos pertinere.' (Ch. xlvi. In Migne's 'Theo. Cursus Compl.,' tom. i., c. 1026.)

The ancient Fathers, indeed, spoke of Christ as *suffering*, *being slain*, and *dying* in the Eucharist And this is good evidence of the sense in which we are to understand their teaching concerning the Eucharistic sacrifice and immolation. See Lombard, 'Sent.,' Lib. IV., Dist. XII., fol. 315b.

Paris, 1558. 'Breviter dici potest, illud quod offertur et consecratur a sacerdote vocari sacrificium et oblationem : quia memoria est et representatio veri sacrificii, et sanctæ immolationis factæ in ara crucis.' (See also Bishop Jewel, ' Harding, Thess.,' pp. 718, 719.)

We are not to transfer such language from the sphere of *representation* into the region of *reality*. The Jesuit Salmeron wrote : ' Quod benigne interpretandum—nimirum, mactationem antiquam Christi in cruce inveniri, non novam et realem ab eâ distinctam. Si in cœna mactatus erat, quomodo ad nonam horam diei usque sequentis vixit ? Absurda hæc sunt, et aliena a veritate.' (Tom. ix., tract 31, § 4. See Morton, ' Instit. of Sacr.,' p. 479. London, 1635.)

NOTE J. (*See* p. 74.)

THE MASS COMPARED TO PRAYER.

So Erasmus : ' This only sacrifice . . . offered up for the living and the dead, when prayers are said for them to the Father through the death of His Son.' (See Du Pin, ' Eccles. Hist. Sixteenth Century,' p. 321. London : 1703), with which compare the words of Gaspar Contarini : ' Unum illud verum sacrificium . . . non sentiunt in singulis orationibus nos offerre Deo Christum, cum dicimus, per Dominum nostrum Jesum Christum, etc.' (Op., p. 358. Paris, 1571.)

So Cassander : ' Quomodo oratio, cujus hoc sacrificium species est, propitiatoria dici potest.' (Op., p. 1000. Paris, 1616.)

Bellarmine (while defending its applicatory efficacy) argues : ' Sicut oratio . . . ex se, et ex proprio officio impetratoria est : sic etiam sacrificium, quod est quædam oratio, ut sic dicam, realis, non verbalis, proprie impetratorium est . . . Christus nunc, nec mereri, nec satisfacere potest, sed solum impetrare : igitur impetratio, propria est hujus sacrificii vis et efficientia.' (' De Miss.,' Lib. II., cap. iv., ' De Contr.,' tom. iii., c. 1053. Ingold., 1601.)

APPENDIX

Compare Pusey: 'That One Sacrifice we plead in every "through Jesus Christ our Lord" with which we end each prayer. . . . In the Holy Eucharist we do in act what in our prayers we do in words.' (' Eirenicon,' p. 28.)

See also Lambertinus, ' De Sacrif. Miss.,' Sectio Prima, § 352. ' Comm.,' p. 135. Petavii, 1745.

On the other hand Lindanus (arguing from the Greek Liturgies): ' Longe diversum est a precibus sacrificium . . . Hinc liqueat . . . incruentam hostiam . . . non ad preces . . . sed ad tremendum illud Mediatoris nostri pertinere sacrificium.' (' Panop. Evang.,' Lib. IV., p. 308. Colon., 1575.)

' Cum autem tantopere contendatis, Missæ sacrificium non esse propitiatorium pro delendis peccatis vivorum aut mortuorum, qua obsecro fronte audetis negare vos idem cum Aerio sentire ?' (*Ibid.*, p. 315.)

Melchior Canus distinguishes between the effect of the Mass-Sacrifice *qua* ' satisfactio,' and *qua* ' impetratio.' ('Op,' p. 433. Petav., 1734.)

www.ingramcontent.com/pod-product-compliance
Lightning Source LLC
Chambersburg PA
CBHW021940160426
43195CB00011B/1159